CR
PROBLE

For a complete list of Management Books 2000 titles,

visit our web-site on http://www.mb2000.com

CREATIVE PROBLEM-SOLVING

David O'Dell

2000

First published in 2001 by Management Books 2000 Ltd
Cowcombe House
Cowcombe Hill
Chalford
Gloucestershire GL6 8HP
Tel. 01285 760 722
Fax. 01285 760 708
E-mail: mb2000@compuserve.com

Printed by Chris Fowler International Ltd, London

British Library Cataloguing in Publication Data is available

ISBN 1-85252-359-X

Contents

1   Definitions and Directions   9

2   The 4P+T Model   21

3   P for Person   27

4   P for Press   65

5   P for Process   72

6   P for Product   80

7   The Use of Tools   96

8   The Competences of Creative Problem Solving
    and How to Improve Them   127

9   Facilitating Creative Problem Solving   144

10 The Inventors Themselves   151

11 Tailpiece   189

Index   191

5

Foreword

Many of us have been faced with a problem and have thought that someone else must have done something about it. We do nothing about it, and then years later see the obvious solution in a shop window or in the market place. We then tap ourselves on the forehead and say, "Now, why didn't I do something about that?"

There are those of us who might go down to the pub and tell everybody the solution to the problem and then, unknowingly, we have lost that idea because of what is technically termed 'disclosure'.

If you tell anybody about your idea, you cannot file for a patent or any other form of copyright, and given that nobody pays you for 'a good idea' – but they might pay you for that piece of paper, the patent – it is no wonder the problem solvers are sometimes prevented from making money out of their bright ideas.

Creative Problem Solving gives you a closer insight into the whole business of fertilising one's own dreams and ideas and will motivate you to leave your fireside chair and go down to the garden shed.

Trevor Baylis
London
February 2001

Acknowledgements

The author wishes to thank the following for their kind permission to publish extracts: The Open University for some of the tools mentioned in their B882 course; the Innovation Unit at the Sunday TImes; the Tomorrow's World Unit at the BBC.

1

Definitions and Directions

'I think there's a world market for maybe five computers.'
Thomas Watson, chairman of IBM, 1943

'When I have arranged a bouquet for the purpose of painting it, I always turn to the other side I did not plan.'
Pierre Auguste Renoir

This book is more about the technical and commercial side of creative problem solving than the artistic, however since the same processes can be applied to enhance both, it is hoped that the contents will appeal to people from all walks of life.

Definitions of:
creativity, innovation and decision making

Try writing the key words of your own definitions before reading further.

There are many definitions of creativity; for example Theresa Amabile's American PhD thesis contains over 300. The British workers, West and Farr, published a longish definition with a 'social' underpinning, namely –

'... the intentional introduction and application within a role, group or organisation of ideas, processes, products or procedures, new to the relevant unit of adoption, designed to specifically benefit the individual, group, organisation or wider society'.

9

Note the acceptance that implementing ideas from elsewhere (sometimes known as idea stealing) also has validity as a form of creativity. However, the most useful definition of creative problem solving is that it involves 'the creation of both novelty and value'.

It is the subtle values implicit within the definitions and/or their logical consequences that can be problematic. For example the inclusion of the term 'of value' in the above definition implies some push to bring the new idea to a wider audience or to the market place in order to realise that value. This infers that scientists will not be content just to use science to understand nature, but that there will be pressures (usually financial) to apply that understanding for some sort of gain.

An example is the debate about genetically modified substances. On the one hand, the history of implementing ideas abounds with examples of conservatism, doubt and outright hostility. Think of Galileo's dangerous idea that the earth might not be at the centre of our solar system. When steam trains first became a physical reality, they were required to have a guard walking in front with a flag to warn members of the public. As plans were announced for larger jumbo jets, concerns grew about the impact of such a large aeroplane crashing on a built-up area.

Each large new idea seems to bring out the worst conservative fuddy-duddies who prefer the comfort of what they already know.

On the other hand, many modern inventions do seem to carry greater and greater risks and the public is becoming angry about cover-ups inspired at the highest levels and organisations that put profit before safety. Examples include BSE and CJD, cracked rails and train crashes, HIV infected blood in France, leaks in the nuclear industry and depleted uranium tips to shells used by the armed forces.

These definitions apply to the creation not only of 'things', i.e. tangible products such as consumer goods, industrial machinery and foods, for example, but would include songs, plays and poetry, as well theories or processes that could be used in fields as diverse as the financial services sector or environmental control as well as to technical or industrial processes.

An important distinction can be made between the terms 'creativity' and 'innovation' and throughout this book the former will be used to indicate producing the novel idea; while innovation will mean the implementation of that idea by bringing it into use. The competences and procedures of creativity and of innovation are very different; for example innovating often requires the painstaking hunt for markets and customers as well as the co-ordination of the finances and means of production. In a larger organisation, not only are there external battles of influence to be won, but also the innovator has internal struggles before the invention starts to breath life. The competences involved in both creating and innovating are covered in detail in chapter 8.

The terms 'problem solving' and 'decision making' are sometimes used almost inter-changeably. In this book however, problem solving will be defined as above, where one is either tracking down the failure of a system to perform as it was designed or is creating something to fit a need.

Decision making on the other hand is a simpler process in which one merely chooses between known or stated options. For example, in a patisserie, one is making the decision to buy either an Eccles cake or a marzipan slice or an éclair or … …

Who is this book for?

Material and references to other sources are included for the following activities and audiences: -

● **Child rearing and parenting**. Parents nowadays play music to their unborn children, hoping to make them more musical. There is no evidence yet that this works, but stimuli that help youngsters become more whole-brained will develop their problem solving. By whole-brained is meant the development of both the left brain (e.g. analytical skills developed by, say, writing and arithmetic) and the right brain (e.g. intuition, seeing the big picture, artistic skills). See also figure 6 for a fuller explanation.

Whole-brained people seem to be better at creative problem solving since the competences involved (chapter 8) require both sets of brain aptitudes. Some parents may have seen the film starring Jodi Foster (single parent bringing up a very bright child) called 'Little man Tate' which portrayed the work of the Odyssey of the Mind Association which aims to help youngsters to become more creative. More details of the Odyssey of the Mind are given at the end of this chapter. There is also the book by Edward de Bono called 'Teach your child to think', published by Penguin.

● **Schools and Universities.** The ideas are for both the teachers and the students.

● **Commerce, industry and non-profit organisations.** This encompasses the largest organisations as well as Parish Councils or Bridge Clubs. There is a view that creativity is largely found in the worlds of art and science. However there are good examples to be found in administrative areas – for example tradable credits were first introduced in the late 1980s. The concept was originally applied to environmental controls such as factory emissions. A factory that was able to exceed governmental controls over, say, the purity of waste water could sell its excess in paper form to another company that was not yet able to comply.

  The UK government is thinking of applying the concept to its future legislation over landfill sites for household rubbish.

● **Private life.** The ideas that follow will also help you in your private life, whether you think of yourself as young or old. When a certain military gentleman reached 65, it was clear that his pension was too low. He started offering restaurants a chicken recipe in exchange for a share in any extra profit. He travelled for two years before the 1,008th restaurant accepted his idea, and Kentucky Fried Chicken had been launched by Colonel Sanders.

Diary time

Whenever you see the above symbol and heading it will signify an opportunity to reflect on what you are hoping to learn and how you can use what you have learned. It is strongly suggested that you write down your responses to the questions (keep a dedicated note pad handy) since writing has a different effect from simply thinking about the question.

Questions What does creativity and problem solving mean to you? Make a list of key words.

Why are you reading this book? Explore your response further by asking 'why' a few more times to get to the heart of the issue.

What do you hope to gain? What might you do differently as a result of having read this book?

 This symbol indicates that some tips for facilitating the processes of problem solving will follow.

Problem solving in its setting

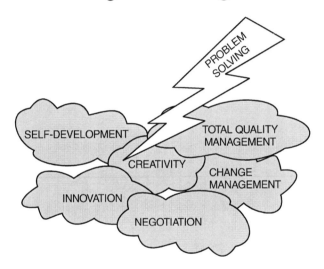

Figure 1 – Problem solving and its environmental context

Figure 1 shows the relationships between the main elements of the environment for problem solving – this book concentrates on creativity and to a lesser extent on innovation. However, if you have worked in any of the other fields you may recognise some of the tools and processes, albeit sometimes with different names. It is clearly not just a higher IQ that leads to more effective problem solving. Indeed, de Bono has warned of the 'intelligence trap' in which the over-use of critical judgement is much less effective than the capacity to help another person improve his or her ideas. In his book, *Multiple Intelligences* (published by Harvard University Press), Gardiner has examples of the creative and problem-solving powers of individuals in many diverse walks of life – he quotes Einstein and Freud for their scientific and social science acumen as well as Gandhi for his political activities, Picasso for his sheer visual creativity and dancers for their artistic and kinetic creativity.

The examples throughout this book and in particular the tools (chapter 7) also attempt to cope with the differing problem-solving needs of individuals, groups and whole organisations.

Government, industry and commerce

These are the big beneficiaries of creative problem solving and organisations in many sectors such as NASA, the British Foreign Office, Bexley Council, Seagrams, Texas Instruments, 3M, Fritolay, IBM, Shell, duPont, Eastman-Kodak, ABN-AMRO and NatWest have recently run specific training events. Fritolay claims to have documented savings of up to $600 million from its creativity training and IBM claims to have saved up to 25% of meeting times while maintaining the same quality of output.

The Apollo 13 space mission involved what is probably the world's best known problem statement: 'Hello, Houston, we have a problem'. The film record of the situation illustrated idea generation under pressure when a group of ground staff worked in a room containing only the items also available to the astronauts, in an attempt to produce a carbon dioxide scrubber.

Placing the Hubble telescope in space was another of NASA's very expensive missions that also almost ended in failure. No one knew why the telescope would not produce sharp images in space but in the subsequent fault-finding phase, the problem was tracked down to the speck of paint that inadvertently ruined the optical spacing and focus that produced the blurred images. Later in their idea-generation phase, the scientists were careful to ensure that no ideas for improvement were rejected out of hand, no matter how 'off the wall' they initially sounded. We will see later how critical it is to be non-judgmental until the evaluation stage has been reached.

A brief history of creative problem solving

It all started in the United States in the 1930s with an advertising consultant called Alex Osborne who first described 'brainstorming' as requiring two separate phases. In the first, 'judgement' should be suspended temporarily to avoid killing off nascent ideas. Some people find it hard to avoid judging and evaluating the ideas of their colleagues. However, on choosing to watch a film such as *ET*, most of us manage to suspend judgement; so indeed it is partly a matter of choice.

Other Americans later expanded Osborne's good idea and added extra phases of problem solving but still required that, in the initial part of each phase, judgement should be suspended to enable a good flow of ideas to emerge – this process is called 'divergent' thinking and will be expanded upon later. The subsequent stage in which evaluation and judgement are deliberately utilised to choose between the ideas and select the best is known as 'convergent' thinking. Many large organisations thought that the divergent brainstorming was an outrageously wild process, but these days it is considered quite acceptable. So there is hope that some of today's more 'off the wall' techniques will in their turn become more widely used as they prove that they can be useful.

In the 1950s, American psychologists started to investigate the mental origins of creativity and tried to devise tests to measure creative capacity. For example, one of the Torrance tests requires participants to produce a list of possible uses for a 'brick' or a 'paper clip'. The listing is judged both by its length (the so-called fluency) and also by the originality of the ideas and the capacity of the subject to jump from one class of ideas to another. Thus a subject who thought that a brick could be used for building houses, bungalows, office blocks, bus shelters, old peoples homes, airports, sea ports would not be judged as original as another subject who jumped to the option of using two bricks to castrate camels.

Critics later felt that Torrance's fluency factor correlated only with the sub-set of imagination and also possibly the capacity to do well in tests – since his questions had to be answered within quite tight time limits. Another American, Guilford, addressed the American Psychological Society in 1950 with a paper entitled 'Creativity' and then published his major findings in 1959 and in his book, *The Structure of the Intellect*, in the mid-1960s.

His powerful contribution was that to be really effective, problem solving required an appreciation of all four of the phases of the 4-diamond model , described in Chapter 2, and not just competence at the third step of idea generation. Guilford also decided that divergent thinking was related to intelligence.

Clearly, if one accepts this problem-solving model, then creativity is more than just divergent thinking. The two complementary patterns of convergent and divergent thinking must run alongside one another. This concept will be examined in detail in chapter 6. However, Guilford's ideas started a useful debate. Several other researchers disagreed and finally, in 1981, Barron and Harrington published their results, which had failed to detect a meaningful correlation between intelligence (essentially IQ) and creative problem solving. Yet other workers argued that it was more the *application* of intelligence that was key to creativity. This explained the observable phenomena that the stereotypical 'nutty' professor may not be as creative – and probably even less innovative – as those in other professions.

Those who actually achieve functioning break-throughs (i.e. implementing novel ideas of value) frequently have a preference for pragmatism and are also likely to have social skills – for example the influencing skills of effective networkers. In multi-functional organisations, one needs the skills to convince the marketers as well as the finance departments and possibly even the operational units of the value of a new idea.

Towards the end of the 1980s, it was broadly accepted that IQ was only part of the story of creativity and that IQ was a necessary but not sufficient condition. The mainstream of investigation then shifted to the identification of traits that correlated with creativity or with innovation. A consensus emerged that a cluster of traits combined to give the capacity to create rather than a single factor. The traits most frequently favoured were – self-confidence, intuition, the capacity to cope with uncertainty, enthusiasm or drive and imagination.

One issue for teachers, managers, or employees trying to improve their creative problem-solving ability is that traits such as intuition are themselves pretty diffuse and hard to pin down. It is for example often defined as 'direct knowing' and seems similar to the insight that some call 'gut feeling'. Maybe it is the sum total of your experience to date, stored partly in the sub-conscious.

Intuition usually comes very quickly and, for those who have learned to trust their inner workings, is accompanied by a strong feeling that they are right or at least on the right track. Because the intuitive thoughts arrive unbidden and spontaneously, they are usually hard to explain, which can be a problem if one is working in a judgmental group of colleagues. However, the author has known several senior managers who rely heavily on what they feel is their intuition and argue that in a busy world it is vital to have the capacity quickly to produce ideas that at least succeed some of the time. These managers are of course assisted by having some positional power and, in busy organisations, there simply are not the resources to test their ideas against other possible courses of action – so they 'get away with it'.

There is a negative side to most traits; this emerges when the person becomes extreme in its application and the trait becomes a weakness rather than strength. You may know colleagues who have strengths in terms of being systematic and orderly; but you may also know people who have an exaggerated or degraded version of orderliness that has become obsessive – they may be seen as neurotic nit-pickers. Another example would be how the positive capacity to evaluate can be degraded into the predictable gain-sayers who criticise everything that others produce. What may happen is that individuals sense and/or get positive feedback that reinforces their view that they have a winning trait; but they then fall into the trap of using that trait in all situations, apparently without considering suitability, and as frequently as possible – even when it clear to others that it is an inappropriate response in that particular situation. They have the same fate as the southpaw who initially does well but does not develop a wider repertoire of punches and becomes a one-punch, left-handed boxer.

Kirton, Eysenck and others have described the social consequences for team building, of trying to motivate individuals with 'opposed' traits to work together – especially when stress levels start to rise, for example, as deadlines approach. This has severe consequences for management teams, project teams and marriages and will be easily recognised by those BBC viewers who watch the parish council meetings shown in the 'Vicar of Dibley'. Accordingly, people rated as 'creative' will often display the traits of vivid imaginations, outspokenness, the ability to challenge and the consequent capacity to withstand the disapproval of their colleagues. However, the negative side of these virtues is that they will often be seen as unreliable, 'difficult' to manage, unruly and untidy. Those individuals who can form a lasting relationship (or a supply of short relationships) with others with contrary traits can learn to act as powerful duo.

From the 1950s, a prolific school of problem solvers was founded at the University of Buffalo in Upper New York State – close to Niagara Falls. From here, Sidney Parnes first published the six step divergent/convergent process model. Since then there have been published many other multi-step problem solving models.

Of interest to readers wishing to improve their creative skills, the Buffalo group run an annual summer school known as the 'Creative problem solving institute' or CPSI. This provides the opportunity to facilitate others in problem solving as well as listening to lectures and taking part in workshops – the content has a very wide appeal and spans from the academic to the spiritual. The event is highly experiential and fun; many of the American stars of problem solving show up; the bookshop is excellent and inexpensive and the event can be attended quite cheaply. The corporate attendees who are paid to attend usually stay at the Hilton but others can stay in student accommodation and eat in the campus refectory. Within Europe, the EACI (European Association of Creativity and Innovation) run a conference every other year in mid-December. It is organised by the Dutch and held in the Netherlands but the delegates are from all over the world.

In the 1940s and '50s, a rather free-flowing approach emerged in the USA and was called 'Synechtics' by its originators WJJ Gordon and GM Prince. For example, in order to stimulate a group of in-house problem solvers, they may invite an outsider to ask the unaskable questions such as 'why are we doing this in this way?' They have techniques such as 'springboards' to energise the groups and to try to stop them solving issues only with conventional methods. As another stimulation they may use an 'excursion' – either in the mind or literally going out of the room in order to seek some fresh approach to the problem or opportunity. However, Synechtics was also businesslike – there was normally a pre-meeting to clarify the problem and the problem owner's needs were always taken as paramount. If you want to read further, see V Nolan's *Innovators' Handbook*, published by Sphere.

In the USA, the creative problem-solving movement has spread from Buffalo – for example to the Centre for Creative Leadership in North Carolina, which is a non-profit organisation with 200 associates (they also have an offshoot in Brussels). There is yet another group in Colorado and several in California. More details of some of the other approaches to creativity are given in chapter 2.

Odyssey of the Mind: creative problem solving for children

This non-profit organisation started in America in 1978 when it launched its first creative problem-solving competition for school-aged children. The association now operates in most countries of the world including China and countries of the former Soviet Union – for example in Siberia. It is also strongly rooted in some of the SHAPE schools in Benelux countries. Odyssey of the Mind, or 'OM' as they call themselves, sells books, videos and teacher packs and has a website. The material is fully professional although it has been carefully adapted for children. For example, the teachers require the students to think about the problem statement and produce a number of ways of looking at it. They then steer the children into an idea generation stage, albeit without using these terms. They run annual competitions for schools and these events have a strong requirement to demonstrate creativity. They also award scholarships to promising children.

The competitions that are open world wide to school children use as near as possible culture-free problems usually associated with the plastic arts or music. The competition usually requires a group of children to perform in public. For example, one year the problem was to make and perform on at least three devices that when combined would play a tune – the event was called 'OM believable music'. The rules required that no commercially available instruments are used, thus pushing the children to produce their own 'devices' based on their own imaginations. Another problem called 'Furs, fins and feathers' required the children to create and present a humourous performance depicting the life of an animal from the animal's perspective. The performance had to include the animal and an interaction between it and one or more human beings. During the performance the animal had to display four feelings or emotions. The time limit for the entire presentation was to be 8 minutes and the materials used could not exceed £25 in value.

The act is judged carefully since winning brings global prestige. For example, there are penalties for any unsportsmanlike behaviour and for any outside assistance – from over-zealous teachers or parents. Often the risk-taking performances are rewarded more highly than students who simply solve the problem. The values of OM have struck a chord with older problem solvers and it has enjoyed corporate support – for example IBM has been a consistent supporter. OM can be reached at POB 547, Glassboro, New Jersey, 08028, USA. Telephone +1- (609) 881-1603.

The way forward

The author is sure you will not expect quick miracles in your problem solving – however some of you will be starting a journey, which will go well beyond this book. As Pasteur (the French biochemist) said, 'luck favours the prepared mind'. The luck of having a significant break-through usually comes to those who have prepared themselves by working hard in that area for some while. It is akin to golfers who get luckier the more they practise! Linus Pauling, who won a Nobel prize for chemistry, said, 'to have a good idea, you need first to have a lot of ideas' – which is at the heart of divergent thinking. So, have a lot of ideas …

2

The 4P + T model

'Who the hell wants to hear actors talk?'
HM Warner, Warner Bros, 1927

' We all agree that your theory is crazy; what divides us is whether it is crazy enough to be correct.'
Niels Bohr, nuclear physicist

In this chapter, a useful mnemonic – 4P+T – applicable to almost any problem solving activity, will be explained. In the following chapter, the first of the Ps (P for person) will be explored in considerable detail. You will thus learn about personal aspects of the problem solver which affect the outcome of creativity and innovation.

The most useful and practical model for problem solving is the **4P+T** model which is illustrated in figure 2. This shows the inter-linking between the four Ps and the T for tools.

The 4 Ps represent the following attributes which are key to creative problem solving:

P for person   There is clear evidence (refs. 1, 3, 4, 5, 7 and 10 at the end of the chapter) that individuals vary in their styles of problem solving and this is explored in greater detail below.

P for process   It is most helpful to have in mind a series of process steps for problem solving to guide one through what at times can seem like a daunting jungle. In addition, the results of research into thinking patterns have produced process guidelines (elaborated in chapter 4) which should be strictly

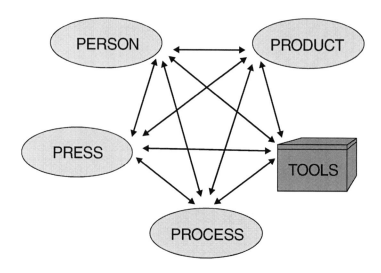

Figure 2 – 4P+T model

adhered to. The key guidelines are the need for periods of divergent thinking (making a list of alternatives) followed by a period of convergent thinking (choosing one or two of the alternatives to carry into the next step of the process). The value of using a process is shown most vividly when problem solving with groups, which is more complicated than working alone, although potentially capable of producing more creative and effective solutions. It improves the alignment in a group to have a common language to describe the need to behave in different ways at different parts of the process and this is described in more detail in chapter 4.

P for product There are some features of the final product of problem solving that can be leveraged to obtain a more effective outcome from the problem solving process. The product or deliverable or result of problem solving can be firstly a material, concrete 'thing', for example, a manufactured article or secondly, it can itself be a process, for example, an improved method for customers or for patients to interact with their bank or GP. In chapter 5, P for product will be explored in detail and it will be found that deliverables which are either things or processes have common features that can be exploited in order to make them more novel and valuable.

P for 'press'   'Press' is the organisational culture or climate that acts as the immediate environment for the other three Ps, i.e. the problem solver, the process and the product. Organisations both deliberately or unknowingly do or neglect to do things that will either help or hinder the problem solving carried out by their staff. In chapter 3, P for press will be explored in greater detail and it will be seen that there are a large number of these organisational commissions and omissions such as providing more or less free time for staff to follow their own ideas, providing trained 'champions' to assist the flow of creative inventions, and providing a creativity room or electronic equivalent with resources to enable staff to grow in their inventiveness. The 'press' can be thought of as a fruit press and it either gently squeezes the creative juices out of you in a benign way, or is more like an instrument of torture such as the mediaeval iron maiden, an iron suit which crushed its victims to death.

 The 4P+T model shown in figure 2 can be very useful to keep in mind either when you are working alone or, perhaps even more importantly, while facilitating a group of problem solvers. The double-headed arrows indicate that <u>each of the five elements can impact on each of the others</u> and this interaction could have positive or negative results. When a group is stuck or even not producing results effectively, the answer usually lies in only one of the five elements – so decide, or ask the group, if the difficulty lies in the tool, or in the process or … or …

One tip is to use the 4P+T mnemonic to design and deliver a problem solving session, ensuring that some emphasis has been allocated to all five elements. Further, if the group becomes stuck the major part of the reason for this stalling is usually to be found in only one or two of the five elements as illustrated in the following examples.

● Firstly, the tool selected may not fit either the process or the people well enough and migrating to a different tool will help to motivate the participants. Usually a structured tool produces the best fit with a well structured problem and vice versa. Also people who like structure (i.e. a preference for analysis, logic and liking to do things in an ordered manner) usually prefer to use structured tools.

- Secondly, when applying P for person; do you know enough about the problem solving styles of the group members? Do you know which group members prefer structured approaches and which do not ? For example, are the Kirton or Myers-Briggs profiles known for the participants? (For explanations about the Kirton and Myers-Briggs approaches see page 34 below.)

  If these profiles vary widely, the group may have difficulties working together especially in the early stages of group formation and/or when stressed. One solution would be to split the group via, say, their Kirton scores into two sub-groups, each more homogeneous with respect to the style of their members. This will make the process less conflictual and will speed it up – however, since the group will lack diversity, the solutions may be less novel.

- Thirdly, when applying P for process, have you yet shown the group a multi-step process model for problem solving such as shown in figure 3, and are they using it sufficiently well ?

Link between the 4P+T model and the '4-diamond' process
The 4-diamond process for solving problems, Figure 3, will be explained more fully in Chapter 4. However, at each of the steps of the 4-diamond process, all five elements of the 4P+T model will apply.

- At each of the four diamonds, one should consider which **tool** will bring the biggest benefit. In particular, in the upper, divergent part of each diamond, you will need a divergent tool for producing a range of options and in the lower, convergent part you will need a convergent tool for evaluating and judging.

- In each diamond, some participants (i.e. P for **person**) will be more effective in the divergent phases and others will be more productive in the convergent phases.

- The impact of the 'P for **press**' of the organisational culture may vary in each of the different diamonds – some organisations seem to push their staff very quickly through the problem analysis stages in order to more quickly reach the implementation stages.

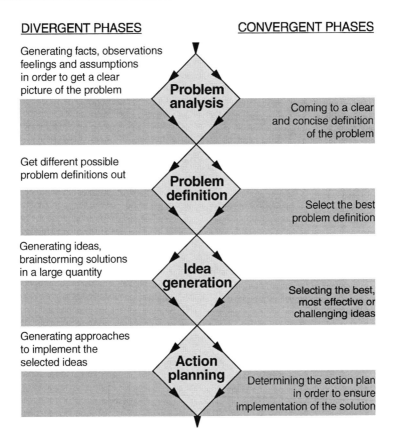

Figure 3 – The 4-diamond model

Other organisations linger for long periods in the initial phases and seemto be suffering from 'analysis paralysis' or 'gold plating'; seemingly unwilling to enter the action planning and implementation stage.

- At no point in the sequence of phases should understanding about and concern for the P for **product** (or service) be ignored. Rarely is a problem-solving exercise completed in the blink of an eye, and during the time lapse, products and services may change or be re-defined. Hence the sequence may need to be adjusted.

- A similar point can be made about P for **process**, i.e. the way things are done. A weather eye must be kept on the whole organisational process to accommodate changes and stay ahead of the game, as well as the actual processes of problem solving.

● In this book, we have defined the step of 'creativity' as *having* ideas, and 'innovation' as *implementing* them. From chapter 8 (Competences), it is clear that these different steps require very different skills and attitudes. Accordingly, since the book was designed to be mainly about creativity, there is not much material on the fourth diamond (figure 3) called 'action planning', but which could also have been named 'innovation'. To correct this imbalance somewhat, I commend the reader to the recent book, *The Age of Innovation* by the Dutchman, Janzen, published by FT/Prentice Hall. With powerful models and a process approach, Janzen guides you smoothly through the technological, market and organisational aspects of bringing new 'products' to market. He also makes use of the 'systems dynamics' approach of which the current author is a devotee.

These aspects of the inter-relationships of the five elements of 4P+T will be examined closely in later chapters.

3

P for person

'People are our key asset.'

Almost every CEO

'Can I have a P please, Bob?'

TV game show

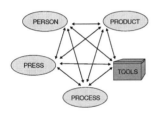

People vary in their approaches to thinking and behaving in such matters as problem solving and this can be measured. Measuring your own style or preference for problem solving is the best place to start an understanding of P for person.

How can you realistically manage, counsel or berate other problem solvers until you have at least an insight into your own approach and its strengths and weaknesses? Most recent approaches to understanding the creative person have been commercialised in that the developer has usually copyrighted a self-scoring questionnaire which is sold together with an explanation of the model, usually in the form of a book. The more helpful versions try to respond to the question, 'so what ?' and give advice on how to apply the results of the style measurement and its underlying theory, to everyday problems and opportunities.

Most of the developers have also added a train-the-trainer module and run courses or workshops to bring outsiders to the level where they can be licensed to run introductory sessions themselves, using the author's materials. These train-the-trainer sessions last for a minimum of two days and in some cases are layered into separate workshops of increasing levels of complexity. After passing some form of evaluation, the would-be trainer is allowed to purchase the questionnaire and other documents that are usually unavailable to the general public. The questionnaires or type indicators or instruments as they are called have been criticised for the usual weaknesses applying to this psychometric approach. For example, some of the questionnaires do not seem to have been fully validated and should therefore be treated with caution. The respondents themselves may fall into the trap of completing the questions in the way that they would *like* to behave rather than the honest – although sometimes painful – way in which they actually behave.

This latter tendency can be overcome to some extent by using questionnaires about oneself, but completed by one or more third parties who know you well. Nearly all the questionnaires currently available examine personality variables; but the author would also like to see an approach based more explicitly on measuring competences. It is arguable that the questionnaire results highlight personality factors that the individual uses to a larger or lesser extent and that these have links to competences; but the linkages are vague and the personality factors are more like personal qualities than competences and the respondent is left without much guidance as to what to do next.

The six major approaches to describing P for person illustrated below all have their own strengths and weaknesses but most problem solvers do not have the time to evaluate these in detail. One approach that the author has observed to work well is where the workshop attendees have some appreciation of the key features of a number of approaches and then select the features that they find most useful for their own portfolio of problem-solving techniques. It is similar to solving the dilemma of which music CD to purchase, which can be resolved by buying the 'Best of' album. All the approaches to understanding problem solving and, in particular, measuring or describing P for person have their own flashes of genius – their 'jewels' and discerning problem solvers gradually build up a collection of these that work well for them in a range of situations.

Some of the author's views of these 'jewels' can be found in the sections below.

 This 'jewel' symbol will flag (<u>underlined</u>) items that are seen as key items in the problem solver's repertoire.

Major approaches to problem solving which have a large element related to P for person.

- Kirton's adaption and innovation theory
- Myers-Briggs type indicator
- Belbin team roles
- Ned Herrmann's whole brain approach
- Edward de Bono's six hats
- Jerry Rhodes and the colours of the mind
- Kepner-Tregoe (KT does not directly describe P for person, but is added here because it is so powerful and has so many features which are complementary to the other six approaches.)

 Every facilitator working with problem solvers should have an in-depth ability to apply at least one of the above approaches. Firstly, they should complete the questionnaire instrument (in the case of Kirton, Myers-Briggs, Belbin, Herrman and Rhodes) on themselves, and have it analysed. Then, having read around the subject (see references at the end of this chapter), facilitators will be able to gauge which preferences or types are being presented in the behaviours of the individuals in the group. This may sound a bit like psycho-babble, but in fact it is quite quick to pick up and is accurate enough to have an impact on the group. The facilitator's challenge is to decide if the behaviour is conducive to the team's efforts at that phase of problem solving. If gauged to be spoiling the process sufficiently, an intervention into the group's process is likely to be necessary. This can be backed up by the relevant aspect of whichever of the above models is being used. If the group's issue is serious enough and/or if the group will meet repeatedly, it may be appropriate to

allow the group members to take the questionnaire and have the background explained to them.

Example 1 – one of the four main elements in Myers-Briggs is the reference for 'judgement', i.e. evaluation, criticism, gainsaying, negativity. From the chapter on P for process, readers will see that, in the early divergent phase of each part of problem-solving, it is vital *not to judge* the contributions of others – that evaluation comes later and is vital in the 'convergent' phase.

Example 2 – In the Kirton approach, the aspect of 'risk taking' can actually be measured. If the facilitator feels that a group is not being adventurous enough, he may want to apply the Kirton instrument so that group members can numerically compare their own risk-taking style with societal data covering thousands of others and also be shown how to analyse the forces that are making them risk-averse or risk-willing.

Kirton's approach

One of the most effective of these approaches is that taken by Professor Michael Kirton (developed at the University of Hertfordshire at Hatfield). Unfortunately the Kirton questionnaire is not in the public domain and you will usually have to pay to receive a measurement and explanation of your problem-solving style. The Kirton approach is worth some study because his instrument both measures what it is supposed to and it does this accurately (ref 1). The resultant scores from the Kirton questionnaire lie on a dipolar scale which ranges from a score of about 40 through a mean (similar to the average) of 96 to higher scores reaching about 160. Scores below the mean are said to have the 'adaptive' style and scores above the mean have the 'innovative' style.

Kirton's early work isolated three variables that influence our problem solving styles:-

1 **'Rule or group conformity'** The extent that we follow or break rules and our reaction to group pressures to conform.

2　**'Sufficiency of originality'** This is not simply the number of ideas that we have but is the number of ideas that we offer for public scrutiny. Some of us (with the adaptive style) operate our own filtering and checking process such that we reject a number of our initial ideas and only make public those that we think are more likely to be successful. It may therefore seem that these 'adaptors' have fewer ideas but that these are of high quality. The adaptive style produces a sufficiency of ideas which immediately seem plausible. 'Innovators' on the other hand produce ideas that tend to be more obviously radical and to produce a proliferation of ideas whether or not they are needed.

3.　**'Efficiency'** A score from the adaptive end of Kirton's continuum is associated with a preference for thoroughness and attention to detail. Conversely, 'innovators' have a broader ranging view but tend to start many things and then get bored with having to follow them through.

'Style' vs. 'Ability'

Kirton argues that **one's style** (that is to say one's preference or approach) **of problem solving does not correlate in any way with one's ability to solve problems**. There are not any accurate measures of this **ability** – IQ does to some extent but not well enough to be useful. So, one can have an extreme Kirton score (have a lot of the adaptive or alternatively of the innovative style) but this does not mean that one is necessarily better or worse at problem solving than someone with a different Kirton score; it is simply that you have a different strategy. This led Kirton, in his book, *Adaptors and Innovators* (ref 1) to state that 'the adaptive style and the innovative style can be equally creative'. However, holders of the different styles can clash especially when a syndicate group or a project or management team is under pressure, and this can lead to conflict.

Clashes between individuals with different styles are more likely to occur between individuals with large differences between their Kirton scores – that is to say between extreme innovators and extreme adaptors. Individuals with a score near the mean of the Kirton scale (scores between about 85 and 105) can, if they wish to accept the task, ✻ **act as peacemakers** or referees between the individuals with significantly higher and lower scores. The author has met people in this range who have been drawn into these situations often without knowing their Kirton profiles and hence not understanding why they were often being called upon to act as an intermediary in group conflicts. They often described these group dynamics as tiring since, with the proximity of their own style to both some adaptors and some innovators, they can sense the driving forces for both parties and may choose to act virtually as a translator between the opposing factions.

Hence the Kirton (or other style measures) can be used for team building – when team members with stylistic differences understand Kirton theory, they usually become more tolerant of the group's diversity. The Kirton instrument has also been used for counselling in long-term relationships. A large difference in style (as measured by any style questionnaire) between yourself and your partner can be a warning that, especially under stress, your relationship may deteriorate into outright violence. However, with the insight that this might be the case, couples can instead learn to use their stylistic diversity to their own advantage. Between them, they can 'cover the water front' in terms of stylistic responses to life's problems and this can be of value. Examples of couples who seem to have managed this are the Thatchers, the Clintons and Torville and Dean.

In a book about the Falklands campaign, there are descriptions of two officers with very different styles or preferences. Brigadier Stapp prided himself on his conscientious approach to his work – even in the stress of battle he tried to remember to let his colleagues and subordinates know where he was and worked long hours to ensure that his administration was up to date – the classical adaptive approach. One of his brother officers was more of the 'dashing' type. During one of the attacks, his unit was becoming stranded for lack of transport. Unexpectedly a helicopter on a different mission flew into range and they persuaded it to land and, despite the pilot's protests, they commandeered the flight for their own purposes. It could have been a brilliant and unorthodox move that in the uncertainty of battle might have delivered a breakthrough. Unfortunately, they overlooked the need to provide flight data to neighbouring units and their helicopter was fired upon by other British troops. For the author, this illustrates the need for adaptive types to practice some innovative behaviours and vice-versa; also for both types to recognise the relative strengths and weaknesses of their colleagues and try (even in the heat of battle) to provide an element of compensation.

Several researchers (Kirton himself and Tudor Rickards of the Manchester Business School) have correlated individuals' Kirton scores with the types of professions in which they (finally) settled – **this approach can therefore be used for occupational guidance.**

From the examples above it can be seen that these thinking style questionnaires can be used at the individual level (for self-discovery and development) and at the group level for team building. The author and others have also used them at the organisational level.

For example, a large multi-national energy company requires different professions to co-operate with their contributions to the entire product life cycle that starts with finding energy and ends with delivering it to the customer. The author discovered a statistically significant difference in the mean Kirton scores of the various professions involved. The initial phase of exploring for energy located under ground requires a relatively large amount of imagination and a preparedness to work with rather ambiguous, unstructured, untouchable situations. This correlates with Kirton's definition of the innovative style but contrasts with the work of, for example, the field engineers, maintainers and production engineers who work in a much more structured, tangible world requiring constant precision and attention to detail (Kirton's adaptive style).

The company had worked hard to prevent the various professions from erecting walls around their activities since the organisation's products and processes were supposed to flow uniformly through the sub-units. Nevertheless, at the professional boundaries, different perspectives and some conflict could still be detected. The Kirton theory delivered an explanation for the stylistic differences and with this came a preparedness to agree that the neighbouring engineers were possibly not trying to disrupt the proceedings deliberately – it was more that they were genetically programmed to react differently and 'couldn't really help themselves'.

The company also had a career development concept that required employees to work for lengthy periods (often years) in very different departments and parts of the organisational process. Not surprisingly, some of these employees later felt that they had certainly not enjoyed these postings – even after they had surmounted the shock of the new occupational culture; they and their managers also complained of lower productivity. It seemed that the gap between their personal styles and their host's professional/ occupational styles (as measured, for example, by Kirton scores) was too large for some individuals to bridge easily and the company later backed away from enforced cross-postings.

Coulter (ref 2) in Canada has researched the different phases of typical project management models and notes that different professions and/or individuals are more effective at different phases and that these correlate with their mean Kirton scores. The Canadians also conceived a continuum of thinking with the need or competence of only low divergence of thought at the one end – for example engineering tasks that are usually routine such as quantity surveying or simple administration. In the middle of their continuum are total quality management type tasks such as seeking the root causes of a problem before implementing solutions. At the high divergence end of their thinking continuum are the really creative paradigm shifts involved in seeing an issue from a brand new perspective.

In an organisational development investigation of a Canadian steel plant, Coulter linked the linear thinking continuum with the typical 'S' shaped curve for the change in growth over time in a typical project management situation. In the industrial situation they even suggested that the project manager be changed three times during a typical project cycle so that the optimum type and quality of thinking could be best fitted to the project needs at that stage.

There is also some evidence that innovators cope better than adaptors with the continuous change that has been such a common feature of organisational life in the 1990s The hope for extreme adaptors is that, armed with this insight, they can prepare themselves better for the white water of non-stop change. Hopefully this lowers the stress that the change would otherwise have caused them and enables them to use their preferred style of creativity to make a more effective contribution to the change processes.

There are statistically significant differences between the mean scores of females and males and the former tend to have the more adaptive styles. Kirton found no meaningful difference in scores between respondents of different ages or ethnic backgrounds. Gender was the only personal variable that he found between respondents and this ties in neatly with the known differences between the brains of the two sexes described below. Other well validated questionnaires such as the Myers-Briggs also produce a difference between the thinking/problem solving of men and women. Care should be taken however to note that this may not apply to any given individual or small group because the sample size will invalidate the statistical inference. Also, women – even in larger numbers – in, say, a technical discipline or organisation may not conform to the statistical patterns since they may have self-selected themselves into those positions. As always, be cautious with statistics – there was once a statistician who drowned in a river whose average depth was two feet – he was unlucky enough to fall into a deep section.

The Myers-Briggs approach to stylistic differences

It is not the intention to give a full explanation of the Myers-Briggs approach here because it is a big subject and also deals with some aspects of the personality unrelated to problem solving. However, readers who want to learn more should consult reference 3. For our purposes, the Myers-Briggs type indicator (MBTI) is a form of questionnaire that gives valuable data scored by oneself or others about how one typically gathers data from the world around and then how one subsequently uses that data to make decisions and solve problems. In terms of data gathering, one is said to have a preference for either 'sensing' or instead using one's 'intuition'. These words have been carefully defined and so do not have the meanings associated with their use in every day conversation. Thus 'sensing' has the following characteristics:

- focus on what is real and actual
- value practical applications
- factual and concrete, notice details
- observe and remember sequentially

- live in the present
- want information step-by-step
- trust experience.

Whereas 'intuition' has the following facets:

- focus on 'big picture' possibilities
- value imaginative insights
- abstract and theoretical
- see patterns and meaning in facts
- look to the future
- around, leap in anywhere
- trust inspiration.

According to Myers-Briggs theory, after gathering data, the subsequent step of decision making is performed with either a preference for the defined terms of 'thinking' or of 'feeling'. Women in general tend to favour decision making by feeling ; but since this is a statistical statement, realise that predictions about small groups of individuals are simply invalid. Solving problems and making decisions by 'thinking' has the following characteristics:

- analytical and logical
- use cause and effect reasoning
- 'tough minded'
- strive for impersonal, objective truth
- fair and reasonable

whereas solving problems and making decisions by 'feeling' has the following facets:

- sympathetic and assess impact on people
- guided by personal values
- 'tender hearted'
- strive for harmony and individual recognition
- compassionate and accepting

The theory further explains that each of us has a dominant mode of operating and this explains why individuals with different 'types' of preferences will have different perspectives on the world. For example Myers-Briggs theory can tell you which of your 'sensing' or 'intuition', or 'thinking' or 'feeling' are your primary (the dominant), secondary, tertiary or quaternary modes. It is **when you are forced to operate in your least preferred (quaternary) mode** that you are most likely to make mistakes and feel more stressed especially if you are required to remain in this mode for periods of months or years. Individuals can usually cope with these differences between them, but when stressed, for example, by time pressure or complexity, the gaps can be quite disconcerting and can lead to conflict. We will see later (ref. 4) that D W MacKinnon in his search for what inspired creative individuals, derived an equation (figure 4) involving the Myers-Briggs variables to explain the differences in creative contributions between individuals.

Figure 4 - Myers-Briggs Creativity Index

MacKinnon's Myers-Briggs Creativity Index

Note - you will need access to your own M-B score to apply MacKinnon's equation, which is:

Creativity = 3(SN)* + JP - EI - 0.5(TF)

* i.e. throughout the equation, insert your 'continuous'** MBTI scores for SN, JP, EI and TF.

Some of MacKinnon's Index results were:

Creative architects	366	
Mathematicians	334	(312 for women)
Creative writers	325	(313 for women)
Research scientists	321	
Californian student average	293	
Medical/engineering students	275	
Orange County residents	225	
Business executives	221	

** You must use MBTI's 'continuous' scores which can be derived from raw scores as follows:
(1) double the difference between the part scores. For E, S, T and J

subtract 1; for I, N, F and P, add 1.

E.g.   S = 20, N = 5   yields 29

    S = 7,   N = 30   yields 47

(2) for E, S, T and J, the continuous score equals 100 <u>minus</u> the above score, but for I, N, F and P, the continuous score is 100 <u>plus</u> the above score.

E.g.   S29 yields 71 as a continuous score to be entered into the creativity index equation, whereas –

    N47 yields 147

Accordingly, MacKinnon's ranking of creativity favours the following MBTI functions:

- With 3 x (SN) score, it favours intuition a lot.
- Plus (JP) favours perceiving (P) types over the judgmental (J) types. This favours divergent thinking over convergent
- Minus (EI) favours extroversion, which the author finds odd.
- Minus 0.5 (TF) favours the thinking preference a little bit and that favours men over women a little.

The Berkeley-based MacKinnon's work can be found in his 1959 paper in the American Journal of Psychology, page 484. In this 11-page article, he discusses the attempts of others to measure creativity. He also discusses the effects of early upbringing and education on a child's creativity – albeit in an American culture.

See also page 60 in this book for a list of attributes of creative people.

The Belbin team role model

The Belbin questionnaire is based on an analysis of groups rather than individuals, although anyone completing the questions will be helped to understand which of the nine roles commonly found in groups is their favourite, which is their second most commonly taken role and so on through the set of group roles. The individual has thus gained insight into their strengths and weaknesses and can decide what to do about these. Belbin argues that sooner or later a problem-solving group will need behavioural inputs associated typically with each

※ role. <u>**If the group knows which roles they are lacking they have the opportunity to be more vigilant**</u> at that stage of problem solving or for individuals to use their secondary roles. The Belbin questionnaire has much face validity and is relatively easy to understand and therefore quick to apply.

Most of the seven major approaches to creative problem solving described here have some similarities and some have been rigorously shown to correlate in a statistical sense (for example, parts of the Kirton and MBTI correlate). One also sees similarities between Kirton's adaptors and Belbin's **team worker** role and between Kirton's innovators and Belbin's roles called **plants** and **resource investigators**. Belbin's approach also fits well with several of the guidelines for effective problem solving. For example, the divergent thinking is often done by the **plants, shapers** and **resource investigators** and the convergent thinking by the **monitor-evaluators** and **finishers.** This is not to say that just because they use this role or thinking mode a lot that they are necessarily effective at it – however, that is for the group to try to resolve.

Ned Herrmann's whole brain approach to P for person

Ned was both a senior engineer in General Electric in the USA and a visual artist and his approach tries to help us to become more whole brained. He spotted that some brain wave plots had four sets of peaks and hypothesised that these were related not only to the two well-known left and right brain hemispheres but also to the two limbic areas. His questionnaire is thus based on clarifying for an individual which of four extreme styles are most frequently adopted in problem solving. His book (ref. 5) is very readable and has many useful tips.

The approach of Edward de Bono to P for person

Somewhat akin to the application of the Kepner-Tregoe approach to problem solving, some of de Bono's most famous contributions (lateral thinking and provocation and movement) really belong to the chapters about P for process and T for tools. However, similar to the Belbin team role approach, de Bono's 'six hats' is aimed at assisting groups of people in collective problem solving. In essence, de Bono has isolated six of the modes of problem solving (for example divergent and convergent thinking) and has named these as six differently coloured hats. Everyone understands hats and the approach provides a common language for thinking and behaving throughout the group to enable it to work in an aligned manner.

For example, part of a meeting plan may state that the group will spend five minutes operating with the red hat followed by five minutes with the black hat. The colour red reminds the members of blood and therefore emotion and thus legitimises the outpouring of emotion – necessary at some stages of problem solving. Analogously, the black hat reminds one of a judge's robes and therefore the need to evaluate ideas as in convergent thinking. It is claimed that IBM put many thousands of their employees through the training package and noted a considerable saving in meeting time together with an improvement in the quality of the meetings. Ref 10 gives details of de Bono's books, one general and one dedicated to the six hats approach.

 The six hats is all about facilitating the problem-solving process. It can be used within the team, dispensing with the need for an external facilitator.

The approach of J D Rhodes – colours of the mind

A simple form of Jerry Rhodes's questionnaire is contained in his book, *The Colours of Your Mind* (ref 7). From this, one learns how one's thinking is coloured red, blue and/or green which correspond with the thinking patterns associated with ascertaining what is (facts), what is right (judgement), and what could be (possibilities). Behind these three primary colours are twenty-one variables that drive the colours, and one's preference for these so called 'thunks' can also be measured. They could also be used as the elements or competences of thinking. Some of **Rhodes's jewels are the 'maps' that he has developed** for several processes such as applying innovation, selling and learning. These maps suggest ideal process steps for achieving these goals that are based upon the thunks or elements of effective thinking.

The Kepner-Tregoe approach to problem solving.

Arguably this section should be included under P for process since the KT approach does not have a questionnaire and says less directly about P for person than the other six approaches. However, it is a big tool and can be very effective (see the ease-value matrix in chapter 6 for an explanation of big and small tools) and contains a lot of 'jewels'. It was developed in the 1940s by the two Americans, Kepner and Tregoe. Like so many Americans, they went together to their garage to invent (like Steve Jobs of Apple computers, like Ms. Graham of the 'Snopake' typing correction fluid). They started by responding to their observations as business consultants that many groups of managers solved problems quite badly and in particular in a rather unsystematic way. They noted that groups of managers very rarely stayed on the same topic long enough to squeeze the value from that aspect and generally hopped around the problem like chickens feeding. The KT approach is very structured and has some very powerful questions that focus on the problem definition and problem analysis phases of the 4-diamond model (figure 3 and explained in more detail in chapter 4). KT is an integrated approach to problem solving in that it almost covers all four phases or diamonds of classical creative problem solving; however it is relatively weaker at idea generation. Practitioners will probably need to import other tools to make effective progress at idea generation. However, KT is again strong at the implementation phase in which it contains a superb contingency plan called the Potential problem (or opportunity) analysis for protecting the innovation from identified risks.

KT defines a 'problem' as an issue where the cause of some deviation (something that is going wrong) is not yet understood. They contrast this with 'decision making' which is more simply deciding between known alternatives. Thus, 'which car should I buy?' is a decision rather than a problem because one is simply choosing between more or less fixed options such as Rover, Ford, Saab etc. This assumes that you can afford one of the brands and know what you want the car for – these latter might however be separate problems in their own right as distinct from the above decisions.

KT used to be associated with technical problem solving especially in the modes of production and maintenance where a process or product slipped from the steady state when a deviation had occurred. However, in recent years with the publication of a revised book (ref. 6) **the approach has been widened both to start up situations where there is no performance history and also to social situations**. The new book contains a large selection of case studies and amongst these are cautionary tales in which otherwise wise management teams have jumped to conclusions about the cause of problems and insufficiently tested hypotheses before pouring in resources for remedial actions doomed to failure.

One such case concerns a large American company that spent some fourteen million dollars and over one year's research effort to try to resolve a fault in a new product that had been insufficiently analysed. A similar lack of rigour in problem analysis spoiled the FBI's attempts to unravel the cause of the catastrophic failure to TWA's flight 800 that fell out of the sky near Long Island. The FBI was under intense pressure to produce results and were tempted to round up the usual suspects – such as Arab terrorists. The FBI appeared to be making progress when they detected small traces of explosives on parts of the wreckage. However, they had chosen to ignore the known fact that the aeroplane had been previously carrying troops in combat gear carrying live ammunition – it would have been more surprising if the wreckage had not contained traces of explosives. They had simply chosen, while under pressure, not to test the hypothesis that the plane had been sabotaged by a bomb.

A lot of KT's power comes from the rigour of the approach – some of their 'jewels' are **the need to distinguish very critically between 'musts' and 'wants'** and to use a numerical weighting method in choosing between options during decision making. Like other methods, KT employs the concept of the problem space – that is the bounded area in which the cause of the problem is said to lie. The cause of the problem is sought as this space is carefully minimised by asking not only 'what is' happening but also operating from the inside of the box to shrink the problem space by also asking 'what is not' happening. They also make the point that so many production problems arise when almost any change is introduced – a change of supplier as well as changes to the process.

The problems whose causes are harder to track down are both the ones that lead to irregular faults as well as those where two or more changes interact to produce an unacceptable result . Shell suffered this latter mode in the 1980s whilst marketing a new fuel – 'Formula Shell'. The fuel's new additives interacted via some complex chemistry with some of the rarer metals used in the construction of existing engine valves. The KT approach was used a lot by NASA and it is claimed that it helped in what followed the words of one of the world's most famous problem statements – 'Houston, we have a problem'. It is said that both the crew of Apollo thirteen and the ground staff were able to work well together because they were both well versed in the same problem solving techniques.

Fiona Patterson's approach to measuring innovation potential

In 1999, Fiona Patterson's work was published in the form of a questionnaire called the 'innovation potential indicator' (IPA) which is sold by the Occupational Psychologists Press (OPP) which is based in Oxford. The work started at Nottingham University and much of the testing was carried out via workshops held at Boots and the Ford motor company. The latter had implemented a significant change management programme, one of whose aims was to help engineers to improve their innovative competences. It is claimed that the work is targeted more at 'innovation' (i.e. implementing novel ideas) than 'creativity' (i.e. having the ideas in the first place). The questionnaire has the significant advantage of being quite short; i.e. only 36 questions (compare with the Myers-Briggs which has over 90 questions in most of its formats) and OPP's guarantee that it has been tested. Akin to Kirton's research, the original exploration behind the IPA used a statistical technique called the analysis of variants. Whereas Kirton detected 3 variables that accounted for most of the variance (i.e. differences) in his observations; Patterson found 4 factors and named these as follows:

1. a motivational effect that was allied with intellectual curiosity
2. a social factor that relates to the capacity to challenge established ideas – this has some similarities with Kirton's factor called rule/group conformity (see section above)
3. a factor related to the style of one's problem solving
4. a preference for achieving implementation in an efficient way.

📖 **Diary time**

Reflect on each of the above approaches.

Questions   Can you see them being used in any of the organisations in which you operate?

How would you plan to introduce the ideas?

Do you need to know more about the approaches yourself first?

What are the benefits of the approach you have selected?

The physiology of thinking

Question – what is our vital friend for creativity? It is superbly packaged, is very economical to run – requiring only carbohydrate fuel and has no obnoxious waste products. It weighs about one and a half kilograms. The answer is of course – the brain.

There has been an explosion recently in the amount we have learned about the brain. For example, some quantum mechanical effects are being invoked to explain some of the very rapid internal transfer mechanisms of data. There are also interesting differences between the structure and functioning of male and female brains. In several respects female brains operate more effectively than their male counterparts.

For example, we all have an organ called the corpus callosum (figure 5) that is situated astride the median between the two brain hemispheres – the so called left and right brains. The corpus callosum acts as a sort of telephone to switch messages between the two hemispheres; however, in women, it operates faster and thus gives women a faster 'whole brain' activity since they can quickly access and integrate data from different regions of their brains. As a man in today's world competing with female colleagues, I would arrive at work earlier, minimise my breaks and stay on later in order to keep up!

In the last ten years, scientists have been able to 'see' the brain at work via a technique called magnetic resonance imagery (MRI). This is a technique in which the minute magnets of the atomic nuclei in the brain's fuel can be forced to resonate with an externally applied

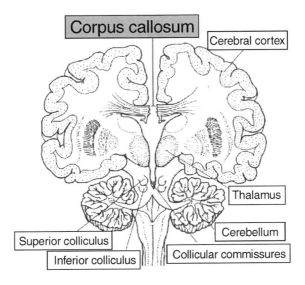

Figure 5 – The corpus callosum

magnetic field and radio signal resulting in pictures of more or less intense colouring which seem to light up to show the areas where the brain is working by actively burning carbohydrate as its fuel. These pictures reinforce the argument that women are able to use their whole brain more effectively than men.

When the same problem is given to both males and females placed in the resonance machine, the women's brains light up in both the left and right hemispheres whereas the men's brains activate mainly on a single side of the brain. Thirty and more years ago it was thought that mental activities were localised in discrete parts of the brain. Thus the term 'left' brained became a popular way of describing the analytical, mechanical, concrete ways of thinking – often associated with masculine thinking patterns (see figure 6). The 'right' brained approach was more holistic, concerned with harmony, possibly intuition and generally associated with feminine approaches.

Although several centres of the brain are now known to be quite localised – speech for example – it is clear that the brain is much more complex and many critical processes are distributed throughout the brain. One metaphor for the brain is to liken it to an orchestra in which

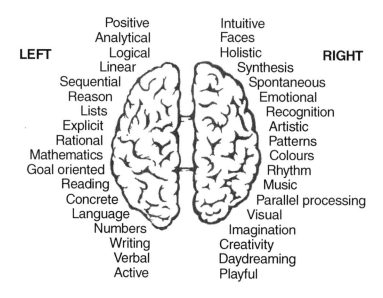

LEFT		RIGHT
Positive	Intuitive	
Analytical	Faces	
Logical	Holistic	
Linear	Synthesis	
Sequential	Spontaneous	
Reason	Emotional	
Lists	Recognition	
Explicit	Artistic	
Rational	Patterns	
Mathematics	Colours	
Goal oriented	Rhythm	
Reading	Music	
Concrete	Parallel processing	
Language	Visual	
Numbers	Imagination	
Writing	Creativity	
Verbal	Daydreaming	
Active	Playful	

Figure 6 – Left and right brain thinking

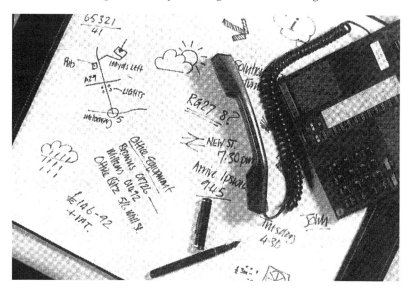

Figure 7 – Doodling

the central mediator conducts the distributed players and synthesises the harmony in concert. These days we still define 'left' brain processes but realise that they are distributed throughout both hemispheres. There is evidence that if the analytic (left) brain processes can be forced to work in a concentrated manner, they can be side-tracked by this focussing which then allows the more harmonious, intuitive, imaginative right brain processes to also produce results. Two examples are those of 'doodling' (see figure 7) and of creative flashes produced whilst completing some mundane task like driving.

Firstly consider doodling and imagine that you are on the telephone talking or probably mainly listening to a boring person; the left brained processes are required to monitor the speaker just in case they say something important or start to terminate the conversation. This frees up the right brain to doodle on a spare scrap of paper – examine your doodles next time, they might contain rare insights to your problems. The same sort of analysis applies to driving (see also 'B' for bus in the section below). The left brain is kept occupied by analysing road signs, avoiding other objects and pedestrians and numerically solving the differential equations involved in accelerating and retarding your vehicle and keeping you safe. The right brain thus escapes from left brain control and muses on whatever seems to be important.

Dominic O'Brian is also known as Mr Memory because he can remember 4,000 random numbers and he can memorise a pack of playing cards in 43 seconds. To achieve this, he somehow lowers his brain frequency to about five hertz – which is the equivalent of being asleep. Professor Susan Greenfield has predicted that before 2020, it will be possible to transplant parts of the human brain – so you will presumably be able to choose between a more male or a more female approach.

Intuition

Intuition is definitely part of one's individual approach to problem solving and used to be associated with a feminine approach to thinking but there seems to be little hard evidence to support this from a statistical viewpoint. Interestingly, *Fortune* magazine interviewed several senior business executives who readily confessed that they frequently used their intuition to resolve complex and/or socio-technical problems. However, they viewed this competence as their own secret weapon and rarely if ever told colleagues about it. Intuition has been defined as direct knowing – and is often described as the feeling that comes, usually unbidden, out of the blue and often with an almost complete solution to your problem. When it arrives, it brings with it a feeling of confidence that the solution is apt and will work. The Myers-Briggs questionnaire described above measures a form of intuition. Books about intuition and how to develop it are given in reference 9.

Brain waves

Several researchers won Nobel prizes by wiring up their colleagues' brains to electrical recording devices and analysing their brain waves. Chief amongst these was the American, Sperry, who produced the sort of charts shown in figure 8.

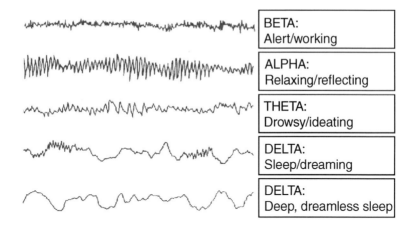

Figure 8 – Brain waves

The beta waves are associated with the brain state known as 'alert and working'. If you would like to experience this state try the experiment shown in figure 10.

Remember to leave a few brain cells free during the experiment in order to monitor your feelings as you complete the task. Take a piece of paper and cover up all the lettering in figure 8 or better still ask a friend to do this for you. Your problem – as your friend slowly lowers the sheet of paper – is to shout out as quickly and as loudly as possible

---

(Note that this experiment cannot be conducted with this actual page. You will need to replicate the five words, drawn quite large, in the colours indicated, on a separate sheet.)

RED (to be written in RED)

BLUE (to be written in GREEN)

GREEN (to be written in RED)

RED (to be written in BLACK)

BLACK (to be written in ORANGE)

Figure 9 – Experience the beta state

the name of the <u>colour</u> that you see. Do not read the word but shout out the name of the colour – in the case of the first word, 'red', it is the same, but thereafter the task becomes trickier. So what reactions do you now have to the alert and working state?

The author has often performed this experiment with engineers who regularly claim never before to have experienced the alert and working feeling! However, one group of engineers also claimed that the brain was a heat exchanger for cooling the blood !

Other brain states
The theta state is often associated with periods of creativity, heightened imagination and lots of ideas. It is commonly experienced as that drowsy, trance-like state felt just before falling asleep and on first waking. It seems similar to the state described by the chemist Kekule as he stared into the glowing embers of a fire. In his reverie his brain was sub-consciously mulling over the problem of the structure of

certain aromatic hydrocarbons like benzene. Chemists of the day thought that, like previously known organic compounds, the aromatics would have linear structures; however, the facts were against this but no one had yet proved how the atoms were joined together.

Kekule himself describes how he imagined three serpents linked in a ring as a metaphor of the benzene molecule and indeed this is how the structure was later found to be. Note that Kekule was not focussing on the problem directly; his 'slow' way of thinking (ref 8) was probably sub-consciously examining the problem from a new perspective that led to the 'eureka' moment of break-through.

There is a model for describing the situations of break-through thinking known as the '5B' model and, in several of these, it seems that brain states like the theta waves are involved.

The 5 'B''s are as follows:
B   for bath
B   for brandy
B   for bed
B   for bus
B   for baby

These Bs describe situations in which worthwhile inventions have been born. New ideas are indeed like premature babies and will need protection and nurture.

B for bath
describes the well-known association between water and creativity. It seems that the creator has to be in physical contact with the water – although as Archimedes demonstrated, the shock of invention may be so exhilarating that one leaps out of the bath and runs down the street. Many people have commented that they also find showers a place for having good ideas. It may be that the warmth and regular massaging of the head by the falling water induces theta waves in the brain.

The story of Susie Metzinger's break-through discovery about immunology also happened in a bath but she was also aided by another creative tool – she was also using a metaphor. Susie had been trying to discover the secrets of the immune response – the body's capacity to sense and then destroy cells found in our bodies that have come from outside. While vital to keep us healthy, this natural mechanism was also hindering the development of tissue transplants. The classical approach was the 'harm' theory that 'self' rejected 'non-self' cells because they were likely to damage the host.

But Susie knew of facts that the existing theory could not easily explain, for example, that we can all eat food as an external and clearly 'non-self' agent and that during pregnancy, women's bodies seemed to be able to switch off the rejection mechanisms in order to retain and even nourish the baby. However, in her bath, Susie was not focussing directly on the problem but was musing about sheep which she kept as a hobby. Her brain seems to have jumped through a number of associations and she was thinking about wolves harassing the sheep. Then, 'eureka!' – she knew that sheep could die from shock when attacked and she started to develop the 'shock' theory of immunology. She postulated that it was the shock of the surgical intervention – often the knife – that led to the cellular initiation of the rejection mechanism. Some of her colleagues have described their state of mind before Susie's break-through as '... only being able to see the old theory in their minds ... like a road that they knew too well ... that prevents them from seeing other possibilities ...'

The conventional wisdom of the dominant group is known as the current paradigm or way of thinking. It is also known as '(co)(w)-(d)un(g)' by those paradigm busters, impatient with old routines. These paradigms are external sources pressurising us to think that there is only one right answer to a given question – the dominant group's right answer. Couple this external pressure with the internal structuring pressure exerted by our own brains and it is little wonder that we find it hard to escape all this structuring and achieve 'out of the box' thinking.

- Around the beginning of the last century, almost every physics professor would have confirmed that heavier-than-air machines would never fly. Luckily, the Wright brothers in North Carolina either did not know this or thought otherwise and, at Kitty Hawk, took their fledgling steps into the air.

- Well before that, one paradigm about the earth was that it was flat – Columbus apparently had two maps of the Atlantic produced by the Greeks, one showed that it was impossible to reach land after setting off in a westerly direction because one would simply not be able to carry enough water together with the other supplies in their small ships. This map Columbus wisely kept to himself – he only shared a second map with his backers and sailors that was more ambiguous and therefore more optimistic about survival.

- Another geographic-religious paradigm was that the earth was at the centre of our solar system. Unfortunately, Gallileo-Gallilei had used his early telescope to observe the heavens and thought otherwise. Sadly for him one of the strongest paradigm traditionalists on this very issue was the Catholic Church. Galileo was ex-communicated and held under house arrest until he publicly recanted his blasphemous views, although it is said that under his breath he mumbled that he still knew it was in fact true that the sun was at the centre of our planetary system. He was only pardoned by the Church in the 1950s.

The history of innovation shows that a certain bloody-mindedness is on occasions a vital way of ignoring the current paradigm. A few centuries later, this was also Marconi's approach in his attempts to send the first electro-magnetic message across the Atlantic. Once again a poll of physics professors would have told Marconi not to bother – it was impossible because it was 'well known' that radio messages travelled in straight lines and that the earth was curved sufficiently that messages could not pass between Cornwall and Newfoundland. The radio waves would instead be transmitted directly into space and lost to mankind. In December 1901, bloody-minded Marconi decided to try anyway and succeeded; the physics professors did not yet know about the ionosphere that reflects radio waves back to earth – and to everyone's astonishment, a new paradigm was born. Another inventor who defied conventional wisdom was the polymer scientist Stephanie Kwolek, who, in 1965, decided to try to spin Kevlar, the strong plastic that is now used in bullet proof vests. Everyone knew that the polymer would not – could not – be spun into filament but she tried it anyway and eventually succeeded. Many of the world's greatest and most novel inventions have come about by their inventors defying the current paradigm.

B for brandy and other intoxicants

It seems reasonable that the euphoria brought on by alcohol produces a brain state that is probably close to the theta state. There is also a class of religious fervours in which people have strong visions. These altered brain states would seem to have non-alcoholic origins – for example, the hermits would have been starved of human inter-action and possibly their nutrition was inadequate. Aldous Huxley has described the euphoric feeling that he knew from singing lustily in church and which he explained as resulting from an excess of carbon dioxide produced by the exercise. Compare this also with the 'jogger's highs' – a euphoric brain state that leads some runners both to have good ideas and become addicted to their exercise. This is said to be caused by the body's own morphine-like chemicals that produce a state of well-being.

B for bed

We have already described how, as the brain starts to drift towards sleep, the theta state is associated with high imagination and creative thoughts. Sleep itself involves the delta state and several creators have been quite clear that they got some of their best ideas from their sleep. Robert Louis Stevenson described the humanoid helpers that he had in his dreams as his 'brownies' and he has written how they helped him to produce plots for his stories. Billy Joel also claims that he got ideas for his songs while sleeping and he has an album called 'The river of dreams'. Isabel Allende, the Chilean Nobel Prize winning author has also been quite explicit that some of her best ideas came from her dreams. On BBC's 'Tomorrow's World' programme in 1996, there was the story of a young inventor who dreamed up the solution to a novel type of fire escape. He had been working for some time on the mechanism but became 'stuck' while trying to produce a solution that was effective but also cheap enough – his dream state produced the novel combination of features, a rope ladder that hooked over the window-sill and could then be thrown out of the window.

B for bus

It is more that the use of *any* transport, rather than just the bus can lead to break-through ideas. It seems that it is the monotony and possibly the gentle but rhythmic vibrations that induce the creative brain state. A study into possible different ethnic cultural origins for different creative propensities showed that statistically the Germans claimed to have more ideas in their cars than elsewhere. The Swiss however claimed that walking gave them their best break-through. Meanwhile, back on the bus – the French mathematician Poincare wrote that he entered a coach in about 1900 with a problem statement in his head and left the coach with the complete solution. He had however not focussed on the problem as such during the journey.

B for baby

The desire to provide for our children has motivated some inventions. This 'B' seems to fall into a different category from the other four; it seems unlikely that the theta state is involved in the cases described below. It seems more likely that it is the profound love for our off-spring that provides the energy to sustain inventors through the trials and tribulations of the innovation process, enabling them to bring their ideas to fruition. Edwin Land, the producer of the Polaroid camera, wrote that the inspiration for the instant camera came to him while on the beach with his daughter. They were taking photographs with a conventional camera – however the young lady wanted to see the photographs 'now, right now!' Land wanted to please his daughter and quite a long while later was also able to delight the whole world. It is also said that part of the inspiration behind the development of the Sony Walkman came from parental love. Certainly there were also major technical factors such as Sony's drive towards miniaturisation that had produced very small loud-speakers that could be placed close to or inside the ears. However, one of the social motivators was that the daughter of one of the project managers wanted to be able to listen to her 'pop' music without intruding on her family who preferred classical music. Her father simply wanted to please his daughter and Sony only saw the Walkman's unique marketing proposition later.

A learning point from the 5 Bs is that, when you feel a serious problem coming on and when you want a novel solution, then go to a place or activity that you know is helpful to the incubation that you need to stimulate or provoke your thinking. This could be aerobics, swimming, fishing, knitting, watching a film or video, or walking the dog.

Do you know what are your most effective incubation past times, or activities or hobbies?

📖 Diary time

> Make a list of what you were doing when you had your best ideas. Are there any patterns?

The incubation of ideas is an interesting part of problem solving as carried into folk lore by such phrases as 'I'll sleep on it' or 'I'll put that report in my top drawer for a while'. It is the process of going 'off line' for a while and deliberately not focussing too hard on the problem directly, but allowing for some provocation or stimulus to direct your thinking into a novel solution.

Guy Claxton has called this 'slow' thinking (ref 8) and contrasts it with everyday thinking at normal speed and 'fast' thinking as exhibited by the rapid responses of athletes such as table tennis or grass court tennis players and musicians such as pianists or violinists playing very fast pieces of music.

One somewhat disputed example of idea incubation is what helped in the RAF dam busters raid during the Second world war which culminated in the destruction of the Moehne and Eider dams. Barnes-Wallis had produced the bouncing bomb that was designed to jump over the nets protecting the dam wall from torpedoes. However, the bomb had to be dropped at night, at a very specific height above the surface of the lake while the planes were under fire.

In the 1940s the RAF's altimeters were also not accurate enough for the precision required. The designers were stuck until one of them took a night off and went to a West-End play. The designer saw how two of the spot-lights sweeping the stage would converge into a single ellipse of illumination on the surface of the stage then – eureka ! elibnis !(the German version of the Greek) or sartori! (the Hindu version) – he had a solution to the problem of how to deliver the bouncing bomb accurately.

Two powerful spot lights were fixed to the lower part of the bomber's fuselage at angles so calculated that their reflections on the lake surface would merge when the bomber was at exactly the right height.

Stress driving out creativity

It seems intuitive that stress will kill our problem solving ability but there is in fact there is an optimum level of arousal or stress.

Too little arousal and we lose the motivation to focus and work the problem. It is unlikely that all individuals have such symmetrical arousal profiles as shown opposite in figure 10 (1). You may know people who wilt at the first stressful encounter (2) whereas others seem to thrive on and indeed require higher levels of stress (3).

Conversely, mind stilling is a technique that you may wish to employ when you are trying to produce novel, creative solutions – indeed it is an integral part of the tool known as 'visual provocation'. It is usually better to sit or lie down. If sitting, let your arms hang loosely by your side or cup one hand gently into the other and do not cross your legs. It is up to you whether or not you close your eyes; you may also wish to ensure that external noise levels are minimised. The key activity is to focus on your breathing and to gradually increase the depth of your breathing. Say to yourself breathe in … hold it for a count of two, three, four … slowly exhale and so on until you are relaxed.

For readers who wish to follow these sorts of techniques, the book *Global Mind Change* by Willis Harman is recommended as well as the book by Marilee Zdenek (ref. 9c). Dr Harman was a well regarded electrical engineer working at Stanford University, who met Edgar

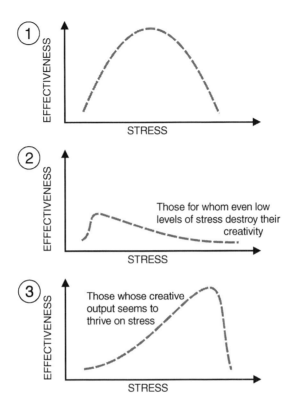

Figure 10 – Levels of stress bearing on effectiveness

Mitchell, the NASA astronaut, who had had a profound experience in space whilst staring back at the Earth. In 1973, Mitchell provided funds to found the Institute of Noetic Sciences near San Francisco and Willis Harman became the institute's leading light.

Harman's books contain several visualisation techniques in which you are encouraged to meet your 'higher self'. See chapter 8 which contains three visualisation exercises for the reader to try. He also suggests that the reader uses affirmations to help them in their lives – this help can take many forms, for example it may help you become more certain that the problem solving path that you are currently on is indeed going to bear fruit.

Although the brain is wonderful, it can lead you astray

It is hoped that you have reconfirmed your belief that the brain is an amazing thing. Its data processing powers alone are phenomenal. For example, if you live for about 80 years, your brain will have processed at least ten terabytes of data, that is 7,142,857,142,860,000 floppy discs full of data.

However, as wonderful as it is, there are some aspects of the brain that you need to be vigilant about. Above all else, the brain is a structure-seeking, structure-forming and structure-retaining entity. In fact, it so good at this structuring that it will even see patterns when they are not really there. Look at figure 11 for a moment and decide what you see in the centre of the diagram.

Most viewers agree that they see a colourless triangle. Of course there is no such triangle. However, the brain in its addiction to structure 'fills in' the bits that seem to be missing.

Instructions

Stare at the centre of the diagram. What do you see?

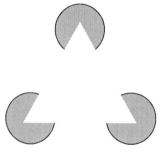

Most people 'see' a colourless triangle, although there is not really any such thing. The brain 'fills in' parts of the image that it thinks should be present. It is this structuring by the brain that can lead us astray.

Figure 11 – 'Structuring' by the brain

For the next experiment ensure that you have a piece of plain paper with you; it can have feint lines on it. Stare at figure 12 with intensity; use every molecule in your body to focus on the picture and count slowly to twenty. Then look at your piece of plain paper and wait for a few seconds to see if you see something.

Figure 12 – The 'eureka! figure

If you see something on the paper, you can say 'aha!' or 'eureka!' to yourself because it is similar to the break-through moment when you suddenly see a solution to your problem for the first time. Of course there was nothing on your piece of paper – but the structure-forming capacity of the mind created something on the sheet. In fact it was your eye in combination with your brain that did the processing; however the eye is generally considered to be a part of the brain, the optic nerves passing directly into the brain. If you have looked at embryos, you will also note that early in their development, the eye-brain complex is strongly associated and it is only at the later stages of development that the brain grows significantly larger.

So, beware – your brain will structure ambiguous situations without your even realising what is happening. However, conversely, you can feel confident that some of the tools that require you to indulge in a provocation or stimulation away from your actual problem will come constructively to a meaningful conclusion. It will be the brain's structuring facility that will bring you back from complex associations and powerful imaginative leaps into more business-like solutions. To misquote Scully and Mulder in the X-files – 'the truth is in there' – you just have to find ways of getting it out of your brain.

Studies into what makes us more or less creative

A summary of the findings of the creativity pioneers such as Guilford, Torrance, MacKinnon and Barron is that the most creative individuals show the following traits.

- **A preparedness to search their environment** – They also have the capacity to spot opportunities.

- **Persistence** – This is most strongly demonstrated as they move from idea generation into the implementation phases of innovation. Thomas Edison eventually patented an effective light bulb, but it required hundreds of failures before he discovered how well tungsten filament worked. However, he somehow maintained his morale and after each failure would note that at least he now knew of another material that did not work. Similarly, Ehrlich, the German biochemist, eventually discovered 'Salvarsan' the anti-malarial drug. He had already discarded nearly eight hundred failures before he had his 'eureka' moment. More recently, Trevor Baylis finally had commercial success with his clock-work radio. However, he faced several years of rejection by entertainment, electrical appliance and battery companies before he was able to find financial backing for his radio. The saying that 'invention is ninety percent perspiration and only ten percent inspiration' is borne out by the examples above and many other case histories of creative people who suffered through the 'long, dark night of the innovator'. See figure 13.

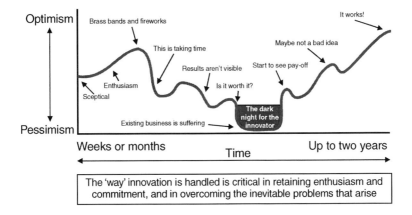

Figure 13 - The dark night of the innovator –
organisational energy during any major transition programme

- **Playfulness** – We know that children can be creative and indeed will often play with the box rather than the toy inside. Children gradually have this creative gift ground out of them by parents, teachers, and supervisors. However, it is this child-like rather than childish state that some inventors are able to maintain or never lose. Einstein wrote that his own childhood seemed so brief that he often tried to hang on to it.

  There is also some evidence of a correlation that creative adults often had an unhappy or stressful childhood. The other characteristic required to make an effective innovator is a certain toughness; enough ego strength to cope with criticism of one's ideas – James Dyson (the inventor of the bagless vacuum cleaner) has said, 'No one feels they have to be nice about me'.

The worthwhile inventions finally transcend the existing paradigms or conventional ways of doing things, although this can take a long time and be painful for the inventor. To market anything new is often to invite resistance to change and, worse, to receive the scorn of one's colleagues.

Ludwig Boltzmann, the Viennese physicist, produced an exciting new approach to thermodynamics involving the then relatively new concepts of entropy and statistical mechanics. Such was the negative reaction from his academic friends that he committed suicide. The final memorial to his greatness was that the thermodynamic equation that he had produced was carved in gold letters on his black marble gravestone.

Another University of Vienna professor, Paul Kammerer, the radical biologist, also committed suicide at about the same time. Although very popular with his students, the bitter in-fighting with his colleagues wore him down. These two cases serve as examples of one aspect of the way that scientific truth is determined at least as much by the social climate of the times as by research logic.

It is worth noting that these early American studies focussed mainly on aspects of **P for person** that led to creativity. In the 1960s and 1970s, researchers such as Theresa Amibile attempted to measure creativity by reference to **P for products** and **P for processes**. However, these approaches have not yielded material that has such pragmatic application. A lot of the work was also distorted by ethnic cultural values, conducted as it was only by Transatlantic workers. In more recent years however some Russian, Central European, Vietnamese and Moslem (Egyptian, Malaysian) studies have appeared (ref 1). Part of the Koran says something like, 'it is good to have many ideas.'

Other factors that correlate well with creativity but have very complex causes and effects are firstly the number of worthwhile inventions produced by recently arrived immigrants. For example in the United States were the Russians Igor Sikorsky (who developed the first commercial helicopters) and Conrad Hubert who invented the hand held torch sold under the brand name 'Ever Ready'. There was also the Hungarian Lazlo Biro who invented the ball point pen that bore his name. Secondly, as shown in figure 14, the number of Jewish Nobel prize winners is most exceptional.

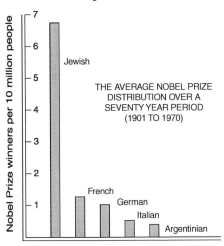

Figure 14 – Nobel Prize winners

References in this chapter

Ref 1   *Adaptors and Innovators* by M.J. Kirton, Routledge, 1992

Ref 2   P. Coulter in personal correspondence with the author, 1998

Ref 3   *Gifts Differing* by I. Briggs Myers and P.B. Myers, Consulting psychologists press, Palo Alto California 1985. This publisher produces many books and documents about the Myers-Briggs approach

Ref 4   D.W. MacKinnon in *The nature and nurture of creative talent;* American Psychologist, 1958, page 484

Ref 5   N. Herrmann, *The Creative Brain;* Herrmann Books

Ref 6   C.H.Kepner and B.B. Tregoe, *The New Rational Manager;* Princeton Research Press, 1981

Ref 7   J.D.Rhodes and S.Thame, *The Colours Of The Mind,* Fontana, 1985

Ref 8   G.Claxton, *Hare Brain Tortoise Mind;* Fourth Estate,1997

Ref 9   Books about intuition:
            R.B. Fuller, *Intuition,* Doubleday

D. Cappon, *Intuition: Harnessing the Hidden Power of the Mind,* York University, Ontario

M. Zdenek, *The Right Brain Experience,* Corgi, 1986

J. Parikh, *Intuition,* Blackwell

Ref 10   E. de Bono, *Serious Creativity,* Harper Collins, 1995

E. de Bono, *Six thinking hats,* Penguin,1990

4

P for 'press'

' If I had thought about it, I wouldn't have done this
experiment. The literature was full of examples
that said you can't do this'
quoted by Spencer Silver, one of the two men
who developed the 'post-it' notepads for 3M

'Chance favours only the prepared mind'
Louis Pasteur

(Isaac Newton is reputed to have worked 17 hours per day for about 10 years.)

📖 Diary time

Questions What things happen in your organisation/family that
a) help and b) hinder creative problem solving?

What would you like to do about these to improve
the situation?

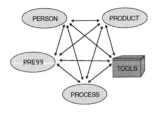

'**Press**' is defined as the organisational
'culture' or 'climate' that effects the
problem solving. There will be things
that happen either formally or
informally and either of these may in
turn help or hinder; there may also be
things that the organisation does not do
that affect the quality of problem solving.

It is also akin to a fruit press which squeezes the creative juices from you. This can either be done like the Iron Maiden – a mediaeval torture instrument – or in a more reasonable and sustainable manner to bring out the best from you. What metaphor would you use for the way in which your organisation induces you to solve problems creatively?

Note that organisational culture is not the same as ethnic or geographic culture. There is indeed evidence that a Scottish introvert behaves more similarly to an Omani introvert than two Scots or two Omanis, one of whom is an extrovert and the other an introvert. Of the many books that examine organisational culture and its effects on creativity the following are recommended – Ross Kantor's *Dancing with Elephants* and *Thriving on Chaos* by Tom Peters.

Examples of 'press'

3M and several IT companies such as Hewlett-Packard have allowed staff up to 10% of their time to develop their own pet ideas. However, there are usually ground rules to regulate this freedom; for example 3M require staff to complete certain core tasks before accessing the 10% of freer time. Another way of stimulating creativity and innovation is to help staff who have ideas, yet cannot obtain development funding from internal or external customers. In 3M, they can apply for central funding. In a similar manner, at one of their R & D centres, Shell have instituted a process called 'Gamechanger' that facilitates the hunt for good ideas and, when an idea has passed certain barriers, the company will provide resources.

Many companies have identified creativity and innovation as key factors in their competence frameworks and provide resources to help employees improve. Some companies (e.g. BP) have gone one step further and provided training in 'managing the creativity of others'. Some companies have established a creativity room or electronic access to resources such as instructions for how to operate up to 20 problem solving tools, books, videos and CDs. A problem-solving room could usefully have an entire wall lined with white boards from knee to head height. This and several flip charts provide the space for writing and drawing ideas whether this be directly onto the boards, onto post-its or onto colour coded hexagons with magnetic strips that adhere to the metal backed white boards. This colour coding can be useful but the availability of large (4 by 4-inch) paper hexagons with re-usable sticky backs has largely superseded the need for magnetic hexagons. It helps to make the problem solving room pleasant to work in – and this could mean providing relaxing or stimulating wall coverings, paintings and music.

Establish creativity 'champions' – senior managers who have been trained to understand the key features of creativity and innovation and have the power to erect a protective umbrella over a project. Boots have established the post of Director of Innovation. It has also been shown to be helpful when leaders publish widely a list of existing problems/opportunities, since it provides a focus for staff to work on and this is the sort of task a champion might undertake.

There are several methods for measuring the organisational culture/climate for creativity and innovation. The questionnaire developed by Ekvall (see chapter 7 in the Open University's *Managing Innovation*, edited by Henry and Walker) is one of the best and it contains some normative data for other organisations operating in various sectors.

It is usually important to reward staff in some way for creating and innovating quality solutions to problems. This need not necessarily be financial but should follow rapidly before the effort has faded from memory. In what ways would you like to be rewarded? Some organisations have instituted 'suggestion schemes' – with or without financial rewards – whereas others see creativity and innovation as a natural part of what they expect from all their employees. Sony has offered cash rewards for the 'best mistake of the month'!! This is not to encourage mistakes, because the mistake has to be written up so that others can avoid making the same error. This approach counters the typical survival response (found in 'punishment' cultures) of trying to hide one's own mistakes.

Although P for press is about organisational culture rather than ethnic cultural differences, there are ethnic effects in problem solving. The Japanese for example call problems 'golden eggs' and welcome them and see them very much as a source of improvements and brand new solutions. Being more community minded than the Europeans or Americans, they will also post a description of a problem in a public space (e.g. the corridor) with the expectation that colleagues will respond by helping them resolve the issue.

Plans to improve an organisation's 'press' for problem solving

One improvement route would be to take the results from a questionnaire such as Ekvall's (see above) and use these to create an action plan. A separate approach or a way of feeding an action plan is to use ideas from an analysis of the other three Ps (person, process and product) and T (tools). Next in frequency after the statement, 'my organisation is not very effective at creative problem solving', an often asked question is, 'which of the Ps provides the best entry point for improvement?'

The first response to this question is, 'entry for what?' The advice is that creative problem solving must be linked strongly to the business needs – it must not become an end in itself. Several organisations have synergistically linked improvements to the three other Ps to existing initiatives. For example, total quality management programmes link very easily because the skills are complementary and some of the tools are similar. Individual and team development issues (covering tools, problem solving processes etc) link well with existing training programmes. Improvement issues arising from a study of P for press usually integrate well with any existing organisation development/effectiveness programmes.

If your organisation is thinking about improvements at the three levels of individual, group and enterprise, this also fits well since problem-solving activities are at the heart of the hour-to-hour life of an organisation. Many of the bigger companies have placed creativity and innovation material on their internal learning webs – for example the Prudential have a web called the 'I'. There are also examples of smaller companies who have achieved a similar improvement with paper-based systems. The author has known initiatives based mainly on spreading the understanding of more problem solving tools or by more selectively focussing on tools for a particular phase of problem solving such as issue identification (e.g. using scenario planning) or the implementation phase of innovation.

Some organisations prefer learning in the classroom (albeit with plenty of worked examples, case studies and lively exercises), others prefer an 'action learning' approach in which participants bring real issues from their work place and solve them in an atmosphere more like a workshop than a formal course. Whatever the mode of learning, it is important to consider how best to transfer the learning back into the job. Helpful transfer techniques are pre- and post-discussions with the boss about the learning targets and presentations on return to work both to one's work team and to a more senior group. Transfer is also helped if the whole team is sent training, partly due to the mutual support that operates on their return. If the application of learning and improvement initiative is well supported by 'transfer' of learning plans, it may be so clear to the organisation that the approach is working well that other time-consuming evaluations of the training or learning are not felt to be necessary.

Global issues of 'press' in problem solving

At the individual level, Kirton (see chapter 2) has not detected any statistically significant differences between the styles of problem solving of different nationalities. However, there are ethnic effects although their causes may be hard to unravel. For example, the number of Jewish Nobel laureates used to exceed those of other nationalities by a factor of 4 or 5 – for data that was collected for the period up to 1970 (see figure 14). This is probably as much connected with the nature and values of Jewish communities and families (a version of P for press) as with the quality of the thinking skills of any individual prize winners. Jewish groups place a serious emphasis on education and have also been subjected to a lot of external pressures and migration; studies of creative talent shows that these sorts of pressures can become converted into a drive for creative talent.

Military conflict seems to create a large number of innovations. It seems likely that this is caused not just by the provision of resources (mainly funding) but also by the motivation to prevail over the enemy. It seems that cold war entities such as NASA can provide the same mix to spur innovation both directly and in spin-off activities. The golden age of British creativity (although not innovation) in the first half of the 20th century may well have had its seeds in Victorian investment. It is also true that centres of excellence are able to attract resources, both finances and people – quality attracts quality. Thus Cambridge science played a part in Britain's golden age in a similar manner to the excellence of Czech tennis and Australian swimming. Britain also benefited from the networking throughout the Empire, e.g. attracting brains to Cambridge, and the fact that the UK acted as a refuge for gifted people keen to flee from the Continent.

 Diary time

Questions   What changes would you like to make to the problem solving 'press' in an organisation of your choice (employer, club, or family)?

Who do you need to help you?

What else do you need?

Examples of organisations that seem to have a healthy 'press' for, creativity

Mention is made elsewhere about the Massachusetts Institute of Technology and in particular of their Media Lab. James Dyson's labs in Wiltshire also seem to have produced a stimulating environment and the Institute for the Future in California also seems to have positive and mellow vibrations. There is the Starlab near Brussels. The MD is Walter de Brouwer aged, 38. He pays salaries up to $200,000 per year which is a good start on the hygiene factors. Their main research targets have the acronym BANG i.e. bits, atoms, neurons and genomes. There is much cultural diversity in the workforce which represents 23 nations and also functional diversity in that 60 scientists represent 48 disciplines. They had a vacancy for a science fiction writer. Amongst the scientists, there are also 30 patent lawyers and money managers. The Starlab's current projects include chopped proteins, attempts to store one bit of information on each atom, heatless computing, nanotechnology, self-assembly processes as accomplished naturally by animal shells and movement faster than light.

5

P for process

' We don't like their sound and guitar music is on the way out.'
quote from Decca Records turning down the Beatles in 1962.

*' I turned my chair to the fire and dozed ... again the atoms
were gambolling before my eyes. This time the smaller groups
kept modestly in the background. My mental eye, rendered
more accurate by repeated visions of this kind, could now
distinguish larger structures of manifold conformation; long
rows, sometimes more closely fitted together; all turning and
twisting in snakelike motion. But look! What was that? One of
the snakes had seized hold of its own tail, and the form
whirled mockingly before my eyes. As if by a flash of
lightening I awoke ... Let us learn to dream.'*
Friedrich August von Kekule (1829-96)
who first proposed the ring structure for benzene

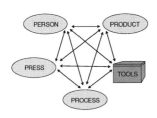

Why is there a need for a process?

Whether solving problems alone or in a group, you really must have a process, i.e. a plan or 'map' of the steps to be followed. This is especially so in a group due to the need to align the talents of the members in a positiveway. A 4-step process as shown in figure 3 (repeated above)

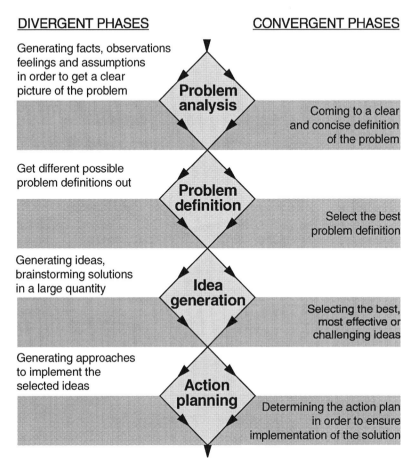

Figure 3 (repeated from page 24)

is strongly recommended. The four phases are problem analysis, problem definition, idea generation and action planning (also known as implementation). If the issue is not quite new, the first two phases may be collapsed into a single step because the analysis of the problem will already have started even if sub-consciously. On the other hand with brand new issues there is a need to start with not so much of a closed diamond as shown in figure 3 – but with more of an open funnel into which facts, feelings, impressions etc can be captured. With a group, this is even more important since large differences in attitude, interpretation and values around the issue will exist over and above differences in facts. The 4-diamond process gives a common language to the group's activities such that with copies of the model on view, all members know what stage the group is at and what sort performance is expected next, e.g. is the group on a divergent or convergent step, or are they about to jump to the next diamond? In the literature, you will find other versions of processes for problem solving – for example with 3, 6 or 8 phases and one bent into a circle to remind you that the process can be on-going.

What do all these process models have in common?

Firstly, they all contain alternating phases of divergent and convergent thinking. Divergent thinking produces as many solutions as possible within the allotted time. People vary in the way they prefer to produce a lot of ideas – some do it by association, i.e. growing one idea from that preceding. Others make larger jumps in which one idea seems to have a very different source or stimulus. The responses to the questions 'How many uses can you think of for a brick (or paper clip)' should produce divergence and a long list with wide differences between the answers clearly indicates an active imagination. Convergent thinking on the other hand requires you to use skills in reality-testing, judgement and evaluation to choose the one or two best options from a number of possibilities.

In creative problem solving, there is a crucial need to separate the divergence from the convergence. Many readers will already know that in brainstorming you should initially withhold judgmental comments. Brainstorming is mainly an idea-generation tool and thus would normally be used at the third phase of the 4-diamond model. However, the strong advice is that all 4 of the phases should have a divergent step followed by a convergent process that decides which options should pass to the next phase.

In chapter 2, it was seen that, in Myers-Briggs terms, some people have a preference for handling data by judging – if this is a strong preference, they may find it difficult to suspend their evaluations during the divergent steps. They may not make judgmental comments but often their non-verbal behaviour will indicate their views. The author has observed a 6-person group in which two members were clearly trying to diverge (i.e. build a list of possibilities), while another pair were obviously converging by trying to choose the best solution from the list – the remaining pair did not seem to know what was required of them. Hence the need for a clear and visible process chart to align the group. Remember also that Linus Pauling – the Nobel prize-winning chemist said, '… that to have good ideas you need lots of ideas'.

Yet another reason for insisting on divergence in your process is to lower the chance of selecting a local minima for your solution.

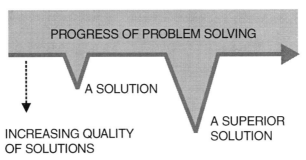

Cross-section through a problem-solving space, showing peaks, troughs, local minima. Assume that a deeper trough means a superior solution. This model is a justification for investing in search processes, in order to find superior solutions.

Figure 15 – Cross-section of a problem

Figure 15 shows an imaginary cross-section running at right angles across a problem-solving model such as shown in figure 3. Let us assume that solutions can lie anywhere in the 'problem space' that forms a box around the direction of advance. Clearly, before recognising a good solution, no one knows whether in general, solutions lie on the line of advance itself or just to one side of it or a long way from the axis. In other words, before the event, you don't know where a good solution lies *in* the problem space or even if a good solution lies *inside or outside* your problem space – which represents the limits of your experience and thinking.

Hence the term, 'thinking out of the box', which really is an exhortation to apply even more divergence in your search. Incidentally this can be one reason for advantageously using groups for problem solving in that the group 'box' of experience is the sum of the individuals' boxes. The central axis of the 4-diamond model can be called the 'motorway of your thoughts' – indicating your progress through creative problem solving. Yet another advantage of being effective at divergence, i.e. getting some distance away from the motorway, is that solutions found far from the motorway should be novel and will give you a commercial advantage in being first to market with your solution. Solutions found on or close to the motorway may be as high a quality as others, but because the motorway is well travelled, they will also more often be found by others.

 It is clearly vital to involve the problem owner in the 4-diamond process. Especially during convergence, the owner should be happy with the choice(s) that have passed through the evaluation. If there is any doubt or, in case of a tied decision, then by definition the problem owner must have the casting vote.

The second important feature of figure 2 is that the first two diamonds are dedicated to clarifying the issue; with a 4-phase model this lavishes 50% of the steps on clarification (this may not mean 50% of your time). This may seem extravagant, but is worthwhile to ensure that the effort to be expended in phases 3 and 4 will be wisely built on firm ground. Einstein said that if he had 1 hour to solve a problem, he would allow 50 minutes to clarify the issues and only 10 minutes for proposing solutions.

 Many of us find the third diamond – idea generation – more exciting than the preceding analytical steps. There is a feeling that one is about to reap a reward with a good solution. Groups of problem solvers also seem to infect themselves with a desire to make concrete progress. It may not be popular, but a facilitator may

have to hold a group back to ensure that they have conducted the first 2 phases well. People will complain that they 'don't have time to analyse the issue to death' – however they may represent those organisations that are able to find the time to go back and complete the analysis properly the second time. Experienced facilitators will not have to be warned about the politicking that can enter organisational problem solving – the hidden agendas that are steering some group members towards their favoured solution. These people will not want to spend too long gathering facts in the initial phases in case the group forms a hypothesis that moves them in another direction altogether. Even apolitical problem solvers may have started early on to form a view of what a good solution might look like. It becomes easier and easier for them to accept data that confirms their initial views and to reject the dissonant data. People always agree that they shouldn't jump to conclusions, but in the heat of problem solving they often will.

Case study

A large chemical company had introduced an expensive new product that was clearly flawed. They had spent a year trying to resolve the problem in which they had spent about £6 million and tied up the activities of their major laboratory. Two of their senior executives were attending a problem solving seminar and, as the importance of the analytical phases was stressed, two bangs were heard as they both slapped themselves on their foreheads – angry at their stupidity in not following a better process.

The third feature of an effective group problem solving process is engendering a positive climate in which members will help each other 'polish' ideas that initially seem mediocre. This is not to say that good solutions cannot arise from constructive conflict, but in the author's experience, it is rarer. The early solutions to problems are often flawed

– they are known as 'intermediate impossibles'. They are like premature babies and they need a lot of help if they are to survive. In extreme cases, these early ideas simply do not work very well (like the first aeroplane); they are usually too expensive to warrant production and they may also have other unwelcome side effects. However, if the basic concept is a break-through, they should justify the polishing that they need to become workable solutions. Groups whose members keep their egos under control during these periods of ambiguity and doubt can achieve more as the following case illustrates.

Case study

In the North of Canada under certain conditions of low temperature and humidity, ice would form on electricity transmission lines and if the ice growth continued, the cable would snap. If this occurred in an isolated area, it was expensive to mend. Accordingly a group of problem solvers was formed to tackle the issue and their dynamics illustrate a number of features conducive to producing powerful solutions.

As the group gathers, they are relaxed (point 1) and exchanging small talk. One member had recently been on holiday in the bush and his family had been harassed by a bear. Instead of simply ignoring the comment, another member builds on the idea (point 2) and jokes 'hey, if we put honey pots on the power pylons, maybe the bears would climb up and somehow dislodge the ice'. This is a classic 'intermediate impossible' and could easily be laughed away. However, another member polishes the crude idea (point 3) and says 'maybe not, but how else could we provide vibration to dislodge the ice?' Now the group has an interesting problem statement. The reader is invited to produce some ideas.

 **Diary time**

Problem statement In how many ways can ice be removed from the power line? In the convergent polishing, find a cheap, reliable method.

Promising ideas that the author has heard are:

Place small windmill sails on the pylons or better still on the power cables. This could be made to work (it seems inexpensive and uses known technology) but needs more polishing. For example, the ice formation often correlates with periods of low wind – but then perhaps the sails could be powered from the electricity within the cable itself …

One idea that skipped over the vibration concept was to use instead the corona heating effect of the electricity flow itself to melt or slow ice growth.

Or … drop bears from helicopters to bounce on the cables!

The most promising idea is to fly a helicopter along the route of the pylons when meteorologists warn that ice is most likely to form.

The first time that you use the 4-diamond model, it may well seem awkward and rather slow. The author's experience however is that the learning curve is rapid and subsequent attempts are a lot quicker. It may help to jot down an indication of time allocations so that the period does not appear open–ended. For example, with a brand new problem, allocate 10 minutes for problem analysis; 15 minutes for problem definition; 25 minutes for idea generation and 10 minutes for action planning. If the group gets stuck they will need some professional help. If group members can articulate their stuckness and agree as to the likely cause then this too can be treated as a problem (or opportunity) and resolutions sought.

Adams in his book *Blockbusting* gives useful advice on 'blocks' and blockbusters and more tips can be found in the chapter about facilitation. Often a coffee break can free up the process and indeed it can be a good design that plans a lunch break or an over-night break into the problem-solving period. 'Incubation' is the term given to the sub-conscious process in which the brain continues to work on the problem even while the body is swimming, walking or dancing – apparently away from the problem.

📖 Diary time

Question	How many times can you remember having a good idea or remembering a name or telephone number while apparently not trying to come up with the answer? Do you have any activity for your incubation that consistently works well for you? (aerobics, fishing, dog walking or … …)

6

'P' for product

'Heavier than air flying machines are impossible.'
Lord Kelvin, president, Royal Society, 1895

'Everything that can be invented has been invented.'
Charles Duell, US patents office, 1899

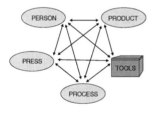

The **'product'** in the 4P+T model is the deliverable or outcome of one's problem-solving efforts and can be a thing (e.g. a physical object like a new type of radio or vacuum cleaner, a theory, a song) or a process. For example, you might invent a new way of achieving something in a technical, administrative, financial, educational or health care field. The environment of the problem solving can be a profit or non-profit making enterprise. In any organisation – whether it is a multi-national or a charity – it helps if the leaders or champions publish a list of any 'products' that the organisation needs.

Companies such as 3M and Rubbermaid have taken this explicit approach even further. In each division, it is required that 25% of sales have to come from products innovated within, say, the last three years. Such tough objectives mean that creativity and innovation cannot remain as some black art that is only practised on away-days. The targets mean that the techniques and tools have to be integrated into the regular patterns of daily life. The staff have to have their 'opportunity spotting' skills switched on at all times so that this becomes second nature to them. Whenever they meet customers, they will be looking for signs or asking about the company's products – 'what works well and what doesn't work so well' – and searching for other market needs that have not yet been satisfied.

The starting point then is to either have some novel technical break-through looking for a market or to have acquired some sense of what the market is looking for or know of existing products that simply do not operate very effectively. Clearly, before significant resources are applied to product development, the problem solver needs to be more certain that the 'problem analysis' and 'problem definition' phases have been completed. In fact the divergent parts of these steps should broaden the scope of the search and possibilities and hopefully produce other options.

The process of clarifying the birth of the 'product' clearly interacts with the organisation's culture for problem solving (i.e. its P for press). For example, does the organisation wish to rely on a smaller but extremely reliable product range or does it want to become more of a conglomerate? Diversification or 'back to basics' move in and out of fashion over quite long life cycles. In the last 30 years, several conglomerates have divested and reverted to core business strengths in a drive to optimise the return to shareholders – for example, Hanson, Shell, and ICI.

Innovating new products is not for the faint-hearted because it is risky, slow and expensive. Studies have shown that up to 46% of an organisation's resources can be funnelled into unsuccessful product development. Also, 35% of product launches fail – often they do not fail in a technical sense in that the product performed as it was designed – however they failed the commercial tests. It is said that in the 1970s, a pharmaceutical company made great cost savings by training pigeons to spot errors in the pills that passed on the conveyor belt in front of them. Unfortunately for the innovation, a rival firm heard about the idea and published an advertisement saying 'would you buy pills passed by pigeons?' Importantly, it has also been shown that in the 80s, 'market pull' profoundly outstripped 'technology push' as a strategy for innovating. Only 21% of product launches could be traced to the latter – that is, having a new approach (or having a novel combination of ideas or technologies) and trying to find a worthwhile market for them. Hence the very real power behind the phrase 'listen to your customers', since they often know what is wrong with your products or service.

Approaches and tools for product development

Firstly, five tools for **divergent** thinking about product.

1. The product improvement check list (PICL)

Van Gundy, in *Structured Approaches to Problem Solving,* has produced a long list of verbs and nouns to act as a stimulant to the reader in modifying or inventing a product. The PICL listing is commercially available via the Buffalo Creative Institute (New York State) or you can make your own list. PICL helps most when you already have a fairly clear idea of what sort of product or product change you want and it is more a matter of scanning a wide range of possibilities. Alternatively you may have an existing product that is not performing as expected, perhaps when operated under new circumstances. For example, taking existing products into space, under water, operating under temperature extremes or in a miniaturised version. The sorts of verbs that should help are somewhat like those provided by the far simpler check lists such as SCAMMPPER or TRANSFORM (see chapter 6) but can be much more expansive e.g. powderise, dilate, dilute etc etc.

2. Morphology (see also chapter 7)

Morphology simply means 'shape' and these techniques use the associative power of symmetry and in particular the novel combinations of ideas to produce results. The author was once requested to assist a team in their search for items they had overlooked. They were producing operating manuals and wanted to be confident that they had covered all the necessary titles. Problems like this are quite difficult to resolve because there are no known tools available. It is also rather like searching for a person with brick-coloured clothes standing in front of a brick wall.

Question. How would you try to solve this problem?

In fact, using the 'magic cube' proved to be an effective approach – see figure 16.

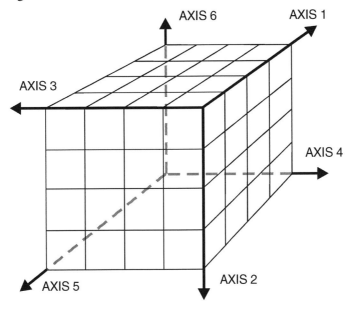

Figure 16 – The 'magic cube'

Firstly, ask the group to define the 5 or 6 key factors central to their work – in this case the operating manuals. Each of these can then be visualised as a vector in a multi-dimensional space – i.e. a cube with six axes. Each of these key factors then becomes the focus for, say, a brainstorm to produce the sub-factors involved. The task then becomes a matter of examining all the combinations of all the factors. This helped the group to see if they had manuals for all of the combinations that they considered viable. The group was responsible for providing advice about the operation of existing plant and the design of future plant and the key factors that they chose were: maintainability, operability (reliability), cost, and health/safety/ environment.

For another example of morphology consider the double hexagon shown in figure 17.

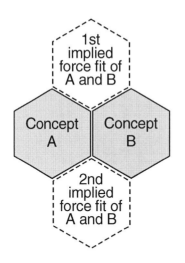

Figure 17 – The double hexagon

Each hexagon represents a concept and it is argued that every pair of concepts is associated with two virtual concepts, which are some combination or association of the two base concepts. In the example given, the base concepts are A 'to ski' and B 'to move over water' – perhaps 'to surf'. One of the combinations of the two base concepts becomes water-skiing, which is already known. However, it is claimed that at the time this tool was used to produce the second virtual combination – 'snow boarding' – the latter was not known and the first entrepreneur to develop the board made a lot of money. Clearly this associative technique employs an initial divergent phase and if a large number of base concepts are used then very large numbers of combinations are produced. The convergent phase involves looking for the golden combination, which has both novelty and value. Since the numbers of combinations can run into the tens of thousands, it is usual to develop simple computer programmes to produce the lists of combinations.

Morphology is a very structured tool and can be derided as very mechanical. However, it has been used in the automotive industry. Mercedes-Benz used the approach to assist in the design of the axle for their E-type range. They used more than three base concepts and analysed over 30,000 concepts. The American auto industry also used morphology to study designs for new carburation systems.

It is the sort of approach that Trevor Baylis could have used in choosing his combination of 'clockwork' and 'radio' when designing appliances designed for the third world. Two of his base concepts would have been 'power sources' and 'type of consumer appliance'. In the expansion of the first base, one would consider mains electricity, battery, wind power, solar energy etc. However, combinations containing these would be dismissed at a later stage because they are too expensive for the third world. The other base concept – consumer appliances – would consider radio, PC, TV, washing machine, premature baby incubator, water purifier, insect killer etc etc. The combination Baylis chose was the clockwork radio and, after a lot of frustration and rejection so typical of innovation, he was finally rewarded and a factory in South Africa is now producing better and better versions. It is rumoured that Baylis is moving on to other combinations that should find markets in not yet developed countries. The production of power in remote locations seems to be a theme for Baylis and one of his latest worthy ideas is the provision of power for land mine detectors. One idea is to tap the energy that is generated in the heel of our shoes as we walk. Another option for powering land mine detectors is to use the energy released when a pendulum swings.

3. Attribute analysis

In its classical form, one analyses the product into its basic components and then replaces these often with cheaper alternatives or with possibilities offering some other unique advantage, such as less maintenance requirement or some other new functionality. In this simple form, the tool does not immediately create novel products but is aimed at producing products that are more desirable in some way. However, as with most tools, the basic version of the approach can be tweaked to enable the jump to a new concept.

Example of the basic procedure for a screwdriver

The components – or attributes – of a traditional screwdriver used to be:
- a handle through which muscle power can be applied
- a straight shaft for engaging the screw head
- a flat blade at the end of the shaft for turning the screw.

See how many more attributes you can think of. Then try varying them to produce as many novel or superior types of combinations of screwdriver as you can.

(**Answer ... did you?** ... add a motor, consider Philips screw heads and Allen key type screws/bolts? Did you consider the offset shaft like a dogleg to enable screws to be turned with very limited access behind the screw head? If you produced yet other combinations, you had better consider selling or developing the idea.)

4. Visioning or wishing new products

The desire to re-invent oneself or one's organisation may involve various visioning techniques. These may be either analytical processes that use for example a SWOT analysis (considering in turn the strengths, weaknesses, opportunities and threats of one's organisation) to build a picture of the preferred niche or innovation. Better still would be demand-lead searches for what the customers would be likely to pay for. Remember that technology-push innovation only accounts for 21% of successful products, whereas market-pull inventions are considerably more successful. A Future Search Conference is a more resource-intensive approach, but also more advantageous – by having more people present, it may start to build more commitment for the future product.

Alternatively, the visioning can be a less analytical process – for example, employees can be asked to envisage future newspaper headlines describing their organisation. In a similar manner 'wishing' is an important part of the synechtics approach which has been described above.

5. The invention machine

This consists of software that can semantically read documents and can then present the would-be inventor with more options for combining into a product than any human could possibly hold in his or her brain or even effectively scan and effectively use on paper. It consists of six elements as follows:

- the product analysis module
- the process analysis module
- the feature transfer module
- the effects module
- the principles module
- the prediction module.

In a simplified way these operate as follows: -

- The **product analyser** defines component functions, evaluates the interactions between components of the system, and by interrogating its databases, proposes ways to increase the value of the system. This assists the user by identifying the key functional requirements of the system and generating high quality problem statements for later manipulation.

- The **process analyser** examines the sequence of technological operations used in manufacturing systems. It achieves this by applying value analysis, cost analysis and function analysis sub-routines to solve process planning and redesign issues.

- The **feature transfer module** improves technological systems by allowing the user to transfer desirable features from one engineering system to another. This enables combination of beneficial engineering sub-systems into a single, hopefully creative solution.

- The **effects module** provides the user with access to over 4,000 animated engineering and scientific effects and examples and selection amongst these is based on the desired functional requirements.

- The **principles module** is a similar type of database in which over 2.5 million patents were analysed.

- The **prediction module** actually solves technical problems involving interactions between objects. This also allows the user to identify key trends in technology with the hope that the user will be able to remain ahead of their competitors.

A recent example included a patent for an electrically heated, quick start catalytic converter to be used in California, which has the world's toughest laws governing car emissions. The company's existing design took six minutes to warm up and become efficient whereas California's green initiative required that catalytic converters become efficient within only one minute. The company's designers had experimented with a blanket-wrapped heater but this required extra parts and had reliability problems. The designers also tried a long, narrow tube that they hoped would increase the mixing of combustion products and thus achieve greater efficiency. By applying the Invention Machine, the team were able to create six more potential solutions, and to streamline the engine design which changed the way they approached the problem – this lead them to examine a variety of temperature-related scientific effects. Using the inventive algorithm, the software identified more then 6,500 examples and scientific laws related to warm-up problems. By converging on some of these options, the team chose an approach based on the fact that certain metals have a temperature-related 'memory', in that they changed shape in a predictable and reproducible way based on temperature. In the combustion zone, a long winding path was created when the metal was cold. The longer path of the gases and increased back pressure would cause a faster warm-up. Once it had reached the operating temperature, the shape-memory metal would 'remember' to straighten, providing the smooth laminar flow necessary for maximum fuel and power efficiency. Such an invention could well be thought of as requiring several weeks to achieve in simply evaluating all the combinations of scientific laws and already patented options. In fact, the team achieved their break-through in only hours. Invention Machine Limited can be contacted in the UK at Milton Keynes on telephone 01908 631123 or via their web site www.invention-machine.co.uk.

Secondly, some tools for **convergent** thinking about product. Most of these tools are concerned with sorting products so that they can subsequently be improved.

6. Voting processes

These are the simplest and have the advantage of being very quick. If N options are displayed – say on a flip chart, participants are given N/3 votes each and simply mark their choices directly onto the chart according to their own criteria. If the group is likely to disagree about the result and/or if the result assumes more importance, it may be necessary to agree the voting criteria in advance.

7. The paired comparison

This method is even more rigorous since it compares each product (or option) against all of the others. However, if you have more than say 30 products, then a paired comparison is quite time consuming and it

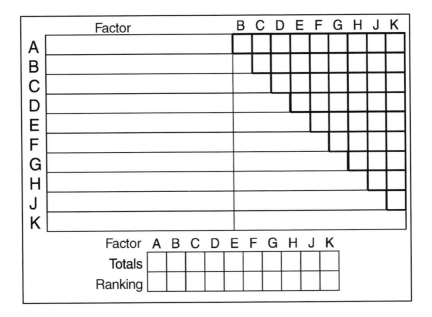

Figure 18 – Paired comparison chart

is usually best to filter the products first on a simple matrix as described below. This matrix can accommodate up to ten factorswhich have to be compared each with every other. A choice between each pair must be made and the favoured letter inserted at the intersection of the two relevant lines. The totals of each letter are then made and a ranking can be devised from those totals, giving preferences and dislikes. To avoid a biased or personally skewed result, do not put your personal favourite as A, but enter it lower down the list. The temptation to choose your favourite, A, against all the others is lessened if it comes up for comparison at intervals.

8. Matrices

There are a large number of matrices that can be used to sort or evaluate products against 2 criteria, which are used as the two axes of the matrix. The effectiveness of the method depends on the relevance of the 2 criteria and for this reason it is usual initially to sort the products against the axes on a purely subjective basis. If the matrix is divided into 4 windows there will always be a favoured or 'golden' window (see figure 18). For clearer comparisons, the matrix can be divided into any number of levels, although a maximum of four in each direction is usually sufficient. This gives a 'golden window' where the optimum answers should lie.

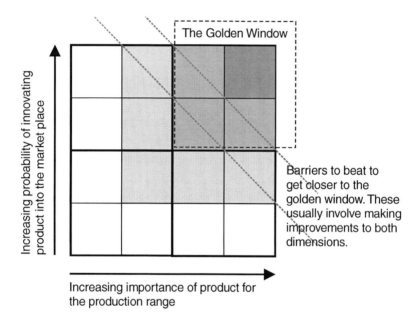

Figure 19 – The golden window

If the distribution of the products across all 4/9/16 windows and in particular the number of products in or close to the golden window is insufficient for product development then the group may have to alter the criteria for the axes – hence the initial sort can be made on a quick and dirty subjective basis without the time consuming use of numbers to score the products. A peculiar or unhelpful distribution of products across the matrix may not mean that the criteria were at fault – it could also mean that the products are just not good enough and need to go back to the drawing board.

As mentioned above, the group should usually choose the sorting criteria according to their own specific circumstances. However, the following are robust pairs of criteria that are frequently independent enough to produce a powerful sorting matrix (the first pair is as shown in the figure above):

- Plot the 'importance' of the product, say, for your product range or because a competitor has already entered the market, against the 'probability of success' in being able to innovate the product to market. Clearly, other choices for the criteria could be 'development cost' or in a second sort it might be 'time required' to reach market.

- Plot the 'originality' of the product against 'realisablity' – very similar to the probability of success. The power of using originality as a criterion in commercial cases is that given success in reaching the market, then the originality should provide patent protection and/or sufficient lead-time to ensure profitability. This is the very essence of creativity – i.e. producing something with novelty and value.

Frequently, there are fewest products in the golden window itself, but this approach can be used to decide which products are most likely to be nudged into this window with least effort or at least cost or whatever criteria is chosen. It is usually hardest to improve products by nudging them across the diagonal of the matrix (since 2 criteria are involved simultaneously). Those with an understanding of the products often get a sense of which boundary (figure 18) of the golden window will be the easiest or cheapest to cross.

Although this approach has been written with commercial terms like market and cost, it can be equally applicable to non-profit products.

📖 Diary time

Exercise   Select a 'product' in your life and apply one of the above approaches to improve it.

Bionics

Bionics is the name given to borrowing ideas for novel products or processes from nature. Mankind has always done this – did the early shape of the bow on a ship come from a plough shape or vice-versa? One of the more recent stories is that the idea for velcro came from the countryside walker who caught a number of burrs in his woollen clothing or his dog or both. The cleverness was to spot the development opportunity rather than to just clean up the inconvenience. Other innovations from nature are said to be the development of heat-seeking missiles from the rattle snake, and the use of a slime produced by some fish that enables then to become more hydrodynamic and thus swim faster. The opportunity here was to coat speciality boat hulls – however, nature still has the upper hand since it knows how to produce the slippery slime cheaply and as an ongoing supply. It was noticed that certain spiders produce very strong web filaments that have been copied as high tensile nylon fibres. Most animals that suck blood, such as vampire bats, also secrete an anti-coagulant in their saliva in order to help the blood to keep flowing. Improvements have been made to the warfarin class of blood thinners that are used by stroke victims.

The list of innovations inspired by an observation of nature is very long – at least 200 recognised products or processes. How many can you think of? Can you spot any advantages in cross-fertilising some of the ideas to make a new concept? Can you also spot classes of similar products and extend the range of these?

As well as being directly inspired by natural phenomena, some inventions have been born from a more general observation of nature. The inventor of the ballpoint pen was allegedly walking through a park on a frosty morning and watched some youngsters rolling a ball down a slope covered in dew. As usual the cleverness was to make the connection between what he saw and the apparently un-connected problem he had of trying to improve the liquid-ink-based fountain pen – the rest was all down hill!

Bluetooth

No discussion of 'product' would be complete without mention of 'bluetooth'. It is a no-wires approach to linking up compatible machines, i.e. machines that contain the bluetooth chip. If you've looked behind your PC or your home stereo recently, you will readily see how it could be tidied up by providing a radio link between the modules instead a physical link with wires. Bluetooth started with Ericssons, the Swedish electronics firm in 1994. They formed the bluetooth special interest group by giving away freely the specifications booklets that had cost millions in research costs. These were offered freely in order to promote an industry-wide standard as quickly as possible.

In 2000, the SIG comprised over 200 companies. Their vision was that the mobile phone could become the heart of a 'personal area network' that wirelessly connects to a headset, credit card reader, palmtop, laptop and/or desktop PC. Their technology is contained within a microchip that, when incorporated within any household or industrial machine, will make it 'bluetooth friendly' and thus enable it to communicate with other enabled machines.

Why would the Swedes want to name their product after a Viking who united Norway and Denmark? As at early 2001, the range between machines is about ten metres, but is expected to rise to 100 metres. The linking radio signal is not line-of-sight dependent and so devices in different rooms or even in outhouses will be able to talk to each other and either issue orders to another machine and/or obey incoming orders. Part of the vision is that intelligent homes will be 'enabled' – for example, the oven or microwave machine will prepare food ready for your return and the central heating will have warmed the house. The intelligent oven will be able to talk to the refrigerator which in turn will be able to order food items from the supermarket. As new items are placed in the 'frig, it will read their bar code and so update its memory on contents and also on the freshness or shelf life of the products.

One potential snag is that the current transmission frequency of bluetooth is the same as as that used by many microwave ovens. A fear is that an oven may be able to give rogue commands all over the intelligent house. One envisages the curtains wildly opening and closing to the strains of Wagner produced by the hi-fi; thousands of pizzas being ordered; mother-in-law being electrocuted etc, etc. If you wish to know more about bluetooth, try the following web sites – **www.bluetooth.com** or **www.ericsson.com/bluetooth.** The intelligent washing machine is already available in the UK. It detects when it has a maintenance issue and uses the internet to arrange for an engineer to carry out a remote diagnosis and perhaps then arrange for a site visit. Merloni is the Italian company that is marketing the model and their machines will incorporate a touch screen, modem and telephone socket for attachment to the internet. The UK support centre that will receive the calls for assistance was operating in mid-2000 and the technology will even identify the parts most likely to be needed in a repair and will order them from a warehouse. It is planned to extend similar technology throughout the full range of household appliances. Electrolux already have a refrigerator that talks to the internet.

Another recent 'product' concept is that of the 'invisible' house – that is one built underground. Make a list of the advantages (such as parking on the roof, better heat and noise insulation, saving space in cities) and disadvantages from your perspective.

Trends in product development

We have already discussed several of the trends which create clothes, machines and other items close to mankind (such as transport) that are more intelligent. Another trend is towards miniaturisation. The electronic revolution of the 1940s that lead from the vacuum valve to the transistor enabled a vast amount of space to be saved. The early satellites that could not carry much payload benefited from these improvements – for example the equipment that first detected the Van Allen radiation belts that surround the Earth and protect us from much of the Sun's deadly emissions. Other examples of 'making things smaller' are the products that must be a nightmare to carry on public transport – the new folding electronic cello and the collapsible carbon fibre vaulter's pole being two cheeky examples. At the extreme end of the miniaturisation spectrum are the advances in nano-technology.

These are the so far simple machines that are about the same size as large molecules. It is possible to make minute screw drivers, wrenches and hammers that could be inserted into the blood stream to repair organs in the body.

'Faster' is also a trend that has seen the gun that now fires at a million rounds per minute as compared with the previous record of about one thousand rounds. The break-through came from a novel form of ignition that was the rate-limiting step in the earlier process. The guns now use electronic ignition rather than percussion.

What other trends can you think of? Can you see a way to achieve a break-through in the technology of your particular industry – perhaps borrowing ideas or advances from another product or area?

7

The Use of Tools

'There is no reason why anyone would want to have a computer in their home.'
Ken Olsen, founder of Digital Equipment Corporation, 1977

'640K ought to be enough for anybody.'
Bill Gates, 1981

Introduction to using tools for solving problems

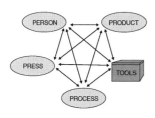

Tools can be thought of as the glue that holds the 4 Ps together (figure 2, chapter 2) in that all the tools have strong links to P for person, P for process, P for product and P for 'press'.The example below illustrates this linkage between tools and P for person. All tools can be ranked in terms of how structured they are (see figure 20). In chapter 2 it has already been shown that people also vary as to how much structure (i.e. order, detail, certainty) they prefer. Accordingly the author has observed on many occasions that for the same problem, one person may love a given tool while a colleague dislikes it, either because it requires too much structure ('… a strait-jacket which didn't allow me my own contribution ….') or because it was too loose.

Link between tools and P for process

Usually tools are simply divergent or convergent although more rarely some larger tools (e.g. Scenarios) cover both types of thinking.

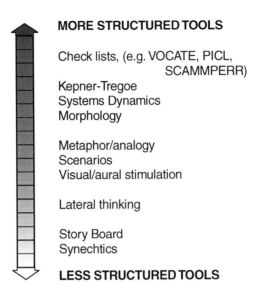

MORE STRUCTURED TOOLS

Check lists, (e.g. VOCATE, PICL,
                      SCAMMPERR)
Kepner-Tregoe
Systems Dynamics
Morphology

Metaphor/analogy
Scenarios
Visual/aural stimulation

Lateral thinking

Story Board
Synechtics

LESS STRUCTURED TOOLS

Figure 20 – Ranking tools by structure

Accordingly the former and simpler tools need to be applied in the corresponding sub-phase of the 4-diamond model (chapter 4). Some tools such as Metaphor are overwhelmingly designed for the divergent stage of, say, idea generation (the third of the diamonds), whereas other divergent tools (e.g. brain-storming or brain-writing) can be adapted for the divergent sub-phase of any of the 4 diamonds. Many tools have a defined scope and are therefore best used within a single phase of the diamond process and this is why readers should develop their own tool kit of favourite tools for each phase. There are however also some tools with a much bigger scope – for example, the Kepner-Tregoe procedure covers all four phases of problem solving.

Link between tools and P for press

When choosing which tool is best suited for any given part of an organisation, the triangle of forces (figure 20) should help the reader make that choice. The concept is that the three (incompatible) forces depicted at the apexes of the triangle are pulling your resultant decision in different directions. The optimum tool for, say, department

X will therefore be a trade off between the different forces. For example, many of the tools are of American origin and may not always be palatable to European audiences, especially when they are new to these forms of problem solving?

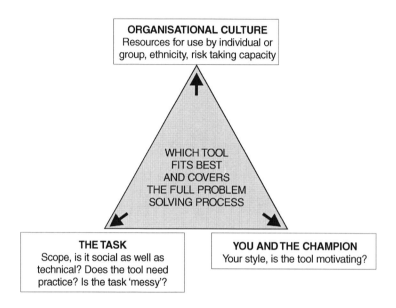

Figure 21 – The triangle of forces

As in engineering there are also tools for designing tools and the Allen morphologizer is an example (see van Gundy's book).

Which tools to start with?

It is suggested that all readers become familiar with one tool for each of the divergent and convergent phases of the first three diamonds of the basic process for problem solving. Tools for the fourth diamond – action planning – are covered later (chapter 7) because this planning and implementation phase is synonymous with innovation rather than creativity. The following tools are suggested for the first three diamonds: -

Tools for the First diamond (problem analysis)

Use the tool known as 'VOCATE' which is a divergent tool, best for issues that are relatively new to you, i.e. that you have not thought through fully yet. The method is based on Systems Thinking concepts – see page 103.

How to apply VOCATE:

The six elements of VOCATE that give it its name are shown below and the key ones are illustrated below that.

Viewpoint:	from what standpoint is the system viewed?
Owner:	who can shut the system down?
Client:	who are the beneficiaries or victims?
Actor(s):	who actually does what is done?
Transformation:	what is actually changed or achieved?
Environment:	what must be taken as read?

Some of these elements need explanation.

- **Viewpoint:** Each observer will have a different viewpoint or perspective of the system, depending on his or her own style, personality, needs, experience, and possibly ethnic culture. The particular viewpoint taken may have a drastic influence on what the observer expects from the system. For example the following are all possible viewpoints of a prison system:
  - a punishment
  - a way of protecting society
  - a mailbag production process
  - an educational system
  - a system to receive, store & despatch prisoners
  - a system to maximise warders' pay
  - a behavioural experiment
  - a system to reform criminals
  - a system to enhance the skills of criminals

If you had looked firstly at the 4th and 7th items, you might not have guessed that the system described was a prison.

● **Transformation:** This is often the most difficult element to apply. If possible, identify which input is converted into which output (inputs can be resources (money, people skills), raw materials, half-converted goods and/or things or processes). If nothing seems to be transformed in your system, you should ask what useful purpose it serves! Also take the following into account:

  • What enters as an input must emerge as a (transformed) output.

  • Different types of input and output should not be mixed. With the exception of the arts, an abstract input cannot easily be transformed into a physical output, e.g. in an airline system, the need for transportation is not transformed into a timetable but rather into a satisfied customer need.

  • Do not confuse the resources used by the transformation with the transformation itself. In the above example, aircraft are not transformed into passengers at destinations. The transformation is : 'passengers wanting to reach A' become 'passengers at A', The aircraft are the resources used.

● **Environment:** There may well be physical/environmental aspects that are important (the system may be in a town or in the country or in a desert, on an island or in the tundra). Additionally, societal aspects may be important – e.g. fiscal or monetary effects such as the tax regime; ethnic values; the use of power or religious tolerance; individuality; or the legal framework, such as local labour laws.

What to do next:
Complete a VOCATE analysis according to the way you see the system now – then complete a second analysis in the way you would like the system to be. Identify leverage points for making improvements between the pairs in these two analyses, i.e. look for exploitable gaps between the two sets of elements in the first and second lists. Gaps that you can exploit in your improvement plan might be either the largest gaps or the most strategic gaps or you may have your own criteria such as the gaps most quickly or cheaply exploited.

What are the benefits of VOCATE?

It is simple to apply, i.e. you can get results immediately, on your own and without prior experience (contrast this with the larger systems tools mentioned in appendix A).

The main benefit is that by forcing a systematic structure on one's thinking about a complicated system, VOCATE helps distinguish the important aspects from the less important. It also ensures that the different viewpoints of the system are made explicit. This can be most valuable when a group of people is conducting the analysis and especially if there is a conflict of views. There is also the possibility of testing the relative strengths of the major viewpoints. Initially all viewpoints are given the same weight and this prevents the person who shouts loudest from imposing his viewpoint on the group. It is also valuable to check the viewpoint(s) with the client or the problem owner early in the process of analysis.

Systems thinking

Systems thinking is usually considered as an advanced creative problem-solving tool – much larger in scope and complexity than VOCATE. Unfortunately it will take you at least 2 days to become effective in its application. and you may prefer to seek an expert facilitator to guide you or your group through its steps. However it is correspondingly much more powerful than VOCATE. It enables you to identify the most powerful feedback loops in your system that can either be exponentially growing or braking. It also has the power to detect any counter-intuitive processes, i.e. steps that you might at first sight think are helpful but are in fact harming your system or vice-versa. There is also the possibility of making a numerical model of your system which can be used to predict the size of flows and outputs and thus test some 'what if' possibilities. This last feature can be an aid in convincing others since in many organisations there is a feeling that 'what can be measured, gets most attention'.To test if you want to find out more about Systems Thinking, the following introductions are recommended.

📖 Read parts of books such *The Fifth Discipline* or (more practically) *The Fifth Discipline Fieldbook* by P Senge et al, published by Doubleday.

📖 The Open University offers the T 241 course on the application of systems thinking. Telephone (UK) 01908 274066 or write to the OU at Walton Hall, Milton Keynes, MK7 6AA. You may not want to take the entire course, but you can watch or listen to modules on BBC television and radio.

Tools for the Second diamond (problem definition)

Divergence:

For the divergent step, use the Problem Box which is best used as an individual tool, but can be adapted for groups. The box itself is depicted in figure 22. This tool is used to explore the heart of the problem and produce a wise definition – what does the problem really mean to the problem owner? The problem box assumes that there is a 'problem space' around the problem. It also assumes that the initial problem statement was probably produced somewhat spontaneously and not rigorously thought out. Additionally there is often resistance to the exploration of the core or root cause of issues and this tool is a good way of pushing through that resistance.

The corollary of this is that this tool works best for new problems. For old problems that have been turned over and over in one's mind, the brain – both consciously and sub-consciously will already have performed the two operations described below and you may not seem to obtain much more insight by applying the Box. It achieves the search process by generating alternatives to the initial problem statement by firstly asking 'why?' in order to explore what is underlying the problem (the same as the 'root cause' in the total quality management approach). You may have to ask 'why?' several times, but stop when the response is, 'to promote peace and harmony throughout the universe'. Secondly ask either 'how?' or better, ask

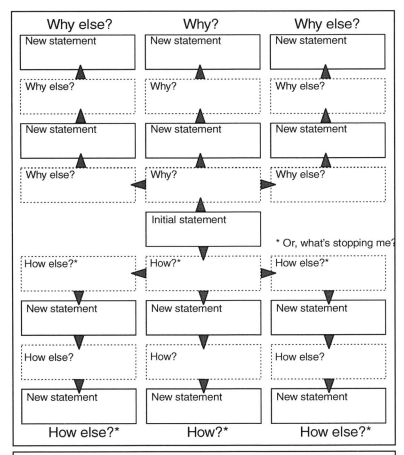

The Problem Box is useful for generating many, varied and unusual problem statements. Start by writing your initial problem statement in the designated, central box. To generate more global, general or abstract problem statements, ask yourself 'why?' you want to solve that problem. Write your answer in the box above the initial statement. Now, turn that answer into a new problem statement and write it in the box above. The same procedure can be used to generate problem statements which are more narrow, specific or concrete by asking the question 'how?' or, better still, 'What's stopping me/us?' Return to the initial problem statement and ask yourself how you might solve the problem. Write the answer in the space under the central box. Now, turn that answer into a new problem statement and write it in the box below your answer. To explore directions that are more abstract or concrete, you can ask yourself 'Why else?' or 'How else?' respectively. This is a divergent tool for problem solving.

Figure 22 – The problem box

'what's stopping you/us?' The latter is often the more powerful since it invokes an action element.

Many problems, especially if they are emergencies, have both a short-term palliative solution which usually deals with the *effects* and a longer-term aspect which involves the hunt for the cause.

Take for example the elderly relative who is complaining that their sitting room has an inch of water on the floor – their problem statement may be 'help me get the water out of here'. However, asking 'why' a few times reveals that the problem does not in fact lie on the ground floor but lies in the hole on the roof. When used in paper format (figure 22) write the initial problem in the central box and write short versions of the responses between the boxes. At each stage, turn these responses back into questions – which in turn become another version of the problem statement. At first, working with both questions and responses may feel a bit awkward but after a while you should be able to skip the intermediate response and move directly from the question to a new version of the question.

If this second problem statement sounds too close to the original question, try exploring the key word in the response in order to obtain new insights/perspectives into the problem.

Let us take another example from the corporate activity of recruiting – assume the original issue was stated as 'how to recruit better employees?' Asking 'why?' might produce the rather mundane response 'because we need more effective people' which however would lead to a second problem statement of 'how to recruit more effective people?' Homing in on the word 'effective' might elicit other responses such as 'how to recruit more creative employees' or '… those that stay longer so that we harvest the value of their training.' The problem has therefore moved from one about recruitment to a hunt for more effective methods of retention, which is a very different issue.

When the overall process slows down, then move to the opposite pole of the box and explore 'what's stopping us?'– possibly returning later to the original area. This tool is especially powerful for issues that have both social and technical aspects. As you might expect after reading the section on P for people, some participants enjoy the Box but others may feel constrained by its apparent rigidity and linear format. The latter should feel free to start with a large blank sheet of paper or to try the tool known as 'brain mapping'.

Example of problem definition

Assume your initial problem statement is: 'in how many ways can the game of football be improved?'

📖 Diary time

Task   See if you can produce at least eight different and workable ideas to improve the game of football. Try using the Problem Box shown in figure 22.

(A range of possible answers is shown at the end of this chapter.)

Convergence:

For individuals rather than groups, the fastest method of convergence is simply to use your intuition as to which aspect(s) of the problem to carry forward to the next diamond. With the Problem Box, one of your versions of the problem statement will usually jump out of the sheet at you with its relevance. If however you have two versions of the problem statement that seem equally relevant, then feel free to carry both forward to the next phase, but be wary of doing this too often because the effort involved in subsequent steps will compound. It could be however that with two statements you have identified a meaningful cleavage in the problem which can be interpreted as dividing the bigger issue into two problems each with their own integrity. It might be of value to ask two sub-groups each to work further on their own preferred interpretation of the problem.

This sub-division may be a matter of deferring the inevitable convergence and if two sub-groups cling strongly to their own perspectives, it might indicate some political motives. Participants who have an inkling that they are not going to like any of the conclusions may well resist the convergence process. The power of many of these tools is that they indeed identify these differences of view, but they will leave you as the facilitator or the problem owner to bring closure to the convergence and complete the process. If more structure to the convergence is desired, choose some criteria for evaluating your choice and even consider scoring these to see which option is the numerically heaviest to carry forward. For groups, some voting procedure is fastest and works well even when participants vote according their various personal criteria. Tell the group that they each have two votes and invite them to register these directly onto the flip chart containing the options. With N options to choose between, a group of 5 or 6 members needs about 3N votes between them.

Tools for the Third diamond (idea generation)
For the **divergent** sub-step, brainstorming is commonly used. One problem however with brainstorming is that it is quite often used (albeit often badly used) and some participants feel bored by it. To pep up your brain storming sessions, read *Creative Thinking and Brainstorming* by J.G. Rawlinson, published by Gower. The following are tips for improving brainstorming sessions – if the group has not met before, start with a quick warm-up possibly using a humourous theme. As the process nears its end, ask the group to each produce at least one 'far out' idea; your exhortation will make it more legitimate to produce some 'off the wall' material.

Alternatively, you could use the non-verbal tool – brainwriting. As well as hopefully being a new experience, this tool also has advantages of levelling the contributions if the group contains both senior and junior participants and if the group contains a fair number of talkative extroverts. It is also useful if the group contains participants from different ethnic cultures. For example, many Far Easterners and to some extent Middle Easterners do not thrive in the rough and tumble of a verbal brainstorm because have been taught that interruption and the shouting of ideas is not a harmonious way to proceed.

How to conduct a brainwriting session
These are best conducted with large post-its; some facilitators like to use magnetic backed cards (often hexagon shaped) but these require a special metal backed (white) board to display them. Hexagon shaped post-its are also available but have no real advantage over rectangular post-its. It may be of value however to use coloured post-its for colour coding – but be quite clear that the advantages outweigh the disadvantages of the added complexity.

Each participant needs a supply of post-its and the agreed problem statement must be displayed prominently, for example on a flip chart. The first step involves the participants in writing their (brief)solutions on separate post-its (only one idea per post-it). After a fixed time limit or as the initial rush of ideas dies down, they are required either to pass their post-its to a colleague or to return them to the centre of the table. In the former mode the ideas pass around the table until all the participants have seen and hopefully added to all the other contributions. In the latter mode the exercise continues as participants then continue to draft their further solutions or examine the ideas of their colleagues. If a colleague's ideas do not spark variations or further ideas then the original wording can be returned unchanged to the central pile. The tool assumes that some synergy will take place and that participants will produce more effective solutions by building on each others' ideas. To ensure clarity and possibly produce some more ideas it will next help to display all the post-its for all to see. Usually they can be simply placed without damage even onto a decorated wall and a clarification step ensues.

For **convergence,** the Golden Window, figure 19, can be used. Alternatively, if all the ideas have already been expressed on post-its, advantage can be taken of this by asking the group to place the post-its into clusters. Each cluster will need an initial title and concepts that seem to fall into more than one cluster should be copied into both. If the overall process is to be taken towards implementation, the facilitator can require participants to decide which cluster they wish to work further on and agree a date by which they will have completed this.

Another **divergent** tool for idea generation is metaphor; this works very well in groups and is usually great fun. Indeed groups that are laughing and exhibiting a lot of energy are usually also producing novel results.

How to use the tool 'Metaphor' (also known as 'analogy')
The purpose of this tool is to use a metaphor to stimulate your thinking away from your actual issue into a new area.

 NB – leave at least 20% of your time for step 6 in which you force fit the 'solutions' from your metaphor back to actual issue in order to find solutions to the latter.

1. Write your **problem statement** for all to see (if time permits apply problem analysis to ensure you have the root problem, re-writing the problem statement as necessary).

2. Select a **motivating metaphor** which can be unconnected with the actual issue. The facilitator may need to give some examples of metaphors such as – 'erecting a tent in a hurricane at night' or 'how to get a cat out of a tree'. The groups may notice that metaphors that are similar to their initial problems are easier to work with but are less likely to produce novel solutions. Alternatively, very different metaphors require a struggle, especially in the final stage of force fitting. However, if the group can cope with this, they are more likely to produce new ideas.

3. List **up to 10 possible causes of problems** in the metaphor, BUT remain in the metaphor (see example below) – be as creative or wild as you like here (1st column in the example below).

4. Write **at least one solution for each cause** – BUT still keep the solutions in the metaphor world. However, if you have a break-through to solutions in the actual problem, make a note of these separately. You may need two scribes if the ideas flow fast.

5. Feel free to **combine any solutions** if they help you to make a new solution. Usually groups are joking, talking loudly and working fast by this stage.

6. **Force fitting**. ENSURE you leave 20% of your time for this step. You have to bend (force) your metaphoric solutions back into your actual problem. For example, assume your initial problem statement was connected with ' increasing profits' and one of your metaphoric solutions was ' washing the dog regularly'. Ask yourselves the following questions.

   (a) What might dog washing have to do with profits? (It might mean that you wanted the organisation to look more attractive e.g. to investors or to customers or to Greenpeace.)
   (b) What do the problem statement and the metaphoric solutions have in common?
   (c) Follow the general direction of both concepts until they collide/mix.

(d) Have these two got any other associations in common?

(e) For both the actual problem statement and the metaphoric solution, change/invert/combine etc their variables (size, temperature, fluidity, time, place, people, energy source etc) until they produce a useful solution to the initial problem.

Example

Step 1 – Identify the actual issue – 'How to recruit higher performing people?'

Step 2 – Metaphors might be 'how to herd cats' or 'how to erect a tent in a hurricane' – but lets take 'how to fish' as a metaphor for recruiting.

STEP 3 - causes of problems in the metaphor	STEP 4 - solutions STILL in the metaphor	STEP 6 - force fitting - back to the RECRUITMENT issue
Ice cover	Dig hole?	Use attraction centre
Don't know if fish are there	Echo sounder	Use head-hunters
Pollution kills fish	???	Improve company image
Predators kill fish	Make protective reef	Better terms and conditions
Too stormy	Go in submarine	Friends and family help to recruit/ persuade recruits
Catch wrong sort of fish	???	Retrain existing employees

Other small tools

The Dispersed Note Book is a divergent tool that is useful when the issue is not time critical and if you wish to involve participants who are geographically dispersed. The tool itself can be used for large groups and can be used in electronic or paper format. The guidelines require that all participants receive a written copy of the pre-agreed problem statement. For the set period of the exercise (say one month) all participants are required to note at least one new idea each day. After say one week the books or e-files are passed to another participant with the hope that after studying the existing ideas and by then combining perspectives, some synergy will result. As before participants are required to continue to make at least one entry per day. The moderator or problem owner will have decided how many times the idea collections are to be passed on, but finally they are returned to the moderator for the convergent process of extracting the best ideas and implementing the next steps. This tool has been used by the author and by staff from the Manchester Business School in industrial settings. The format of the note book or electronic version should be made as interesting as possible and an example is given in figure 23 – in the paper version the author had the format printed on sheets of different coloured paper and bound into a simple booklet.

Figure 23 – Dispersed note book page

By and large you will be better served using 'big' tools for big problems and the smaller tools for lesser issues. In the sections below will be presented a range of 'quick' tools for handling smaller issues and then finally some of the bigger tools will be presented.

Quick tools For Problem Analysis

Meta-plan (also known as 'fast-track')

This tool is for involving the total group in problem analysis.

- Start with a very broad problem statement, for example, 'What are the main issues connected with xyz?' (Use general wording designed to capture both positive and negative aspects.)
- Write ideas on post-its.
- It is best if all group members stand at the board/chart – this maintains energy.
- Name each cluster and possibly prioritise them.
- Individuals may volunteer to work further on a given cluster.

Advantages: Participants are writing ideas in parallel; ideas are relatively anonymous so rank has less power; everyone has a say; it is harder for extroverts to dominate.

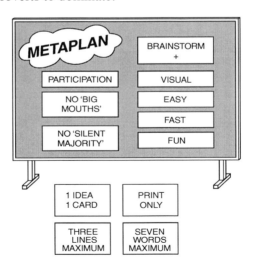

Figure 24 (a) – Metaplan principles

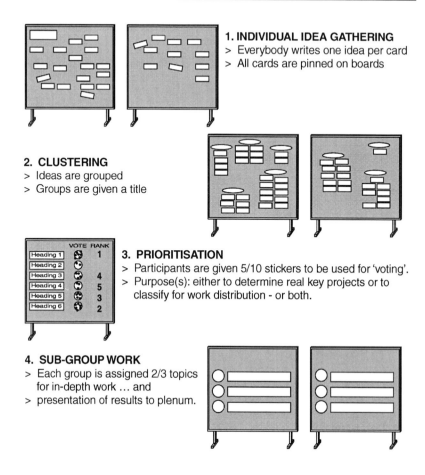

1. INDIVIDUAL IDEA GATHERING
> Everybody writes one idea per card
> All cards are pinned on boards

2. CLUSTERING
> Ideas are grouped
> Groups are given a title

3. PRIORITISATION
> Participants are given 5/10 stickers to be used for 'voting'.
> Purpose(s): either to determine real key projects or to classify for work distribution - or both.

4. SUB-GROUP WORK
> Each group is assigned 2/3 topics for in-depth work ... and
> presentation of results to plenum.

Figure 24 – Metaplan details

Force field analysis (FFA)

This is an individual or group tool, for quick analysis and prioritisation 'for' or 'against' some proposal or forces that 'hinder' or 'help' some aspect. See figure 25.

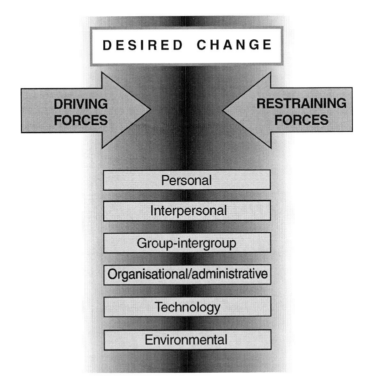

Figure 25 – Force Field Analysis

Force field analysis is a technique for analysing and solving complex problems. It is a tool for studying a situation that you want to change. The method was first described by Kurt Lewin and is based on the observation that, in general, a situation can be described as a balance between two types of forces – restraining forces (those that are resisting the change) and driving forces (those that are promoting or supporting the change).

First, the forces on both sides must be identified. Then they must be weighed in terms of the amount of force they exert. When we can see more clearly what these various forces are and how significant (or strong) they are, there is a better chance of bringing about change in the direction we seek.

We can bring about change in two ways: by increasing the force prompting change or by reducing the forces resisting change. The most effective way is to add to the driving forces and, at the same time, to weaken the resisting forces.

Select a problem that you feel really needs to be solved. If possible, it should be something that has given you cause for concern and that would lead to significant improvement if solved. Choose a problem for which a solution is possible, though difficult. Then work through the following steps.

1. Identify the problem as you see it now.

2. Define the problem in terms of (a) the present situation and (b) the situation you would like to see when the problem is solved.

3. Make a list of the forces working against your desired change (resisting forces) and a list of those forces working in your favour (driving forces). These forces can be related to areas such as people, money, time, external factors, etc – anything that could hinder or help you to make a change. It is not necessary (or desirable) to find balancing forces in each area. Often one area will have mighty forces pushing in one direction only. Balance/imbalance overall is probably due to a similarly large force pushing against it, but is a different category. When identifying forces, it is helpful to be specific and to draw a force field diagram, as shown later, naming the person/people who control the force where you can.

4. Estimate the relative strength of each force. (One method is to draw stronger forces as longer or fatter arrows.)

5. Eliminate those over which you have no control.

6. For each resisting force, list the actions you would take that could possibly reduce or eliminate the force.

7. For each driving force, list the actions you could take that could possibly increase the force.

8. Determine the most promising steps you could take toward solving the problem and identify the resources to help you.

9. Re-examine your steps and put them into a sequence, omitting any that do not seem to fit your overall goals.

This tool is particularly useful where the problem is not so much one of making a considered decision from a group of possibilities, as trying to resolve a 'stuck' situation where the route out of the impasse seems hard to define.

Cause and effect diagram (also known as **Fishbone** or **Ishikawa diagram**)

This is an individual or group tool used for tracking down the 'cause' of some problem. There are several acronyms for investigating commonly occurring possible causes or the possibilities can be brainstormed or brainwritten (use post-its). For a worked example of the tool see figure 26.

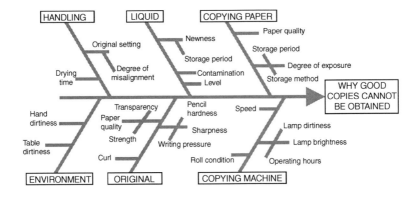

Figure 26 – Cause and effect diagram

Construction of cause and effect diagrams follows a logical pattern.

1. Brainstorm the 'main causes' (in the boxes) using:

   - 4 Ws – What, why, when, where?
   - 5 Ms (manufacturing) – Manpower, materials, methods, machines, measurements
   - 5 Ps (services) – People (employees, contractors), provisions (supplies), procedures, place (environment), patrons (customers)

2. Add further causes to each main area (ensure they really are causes!)

3. Add subsidiary causes.

4. Continue adding causes until each branch has a 'root cause' – something that is controllable.

5. Check the logical validity of the causal chains.

6. Is there a need to test the conclusion?

5 Ws + H (what, where, who, why, when and how)

You may also ask these six questions in the negative. For example 'What is not occurring on this occasion that we might have expected to have occurred?'

Checklists such as SCAMMPERR, TRANSFORM

These can be applied very easily and committed quite quickly to memory. The acronym SCAMMPERR stands for the operations – **S**ubstitute, **C**ombine, **A**dapt, **M**agnify or **M**inify, **M**odify, **P**ut to other uses, **E**liminate, **R**e-arrange and **R**everse.

The second acronym – TRANSFORM is very similar and you may only wish to commit one of them to memory. Here, the letters stand for the following actions to be performed on your product or problem: – **T**wist or **T**urn, **R**everse or **R**otate, **A**dapt, **N**ovelise, **S**ubstitute, **F**use, **O**mit, **R**e-arrange and **M**agnify. Some readers may find these acronyms rather too simple – however the author has known senior managers who thought that their simplicity was their strength, since they could remember them easily and apply them almost automatically in everyday situations.

Big tools

A potentially 'big' problem-solving tool for exploring the future and constructing a strategy for coping with it is Scenario Building.

In its sophisticated versions, a panel of experts will examine the target year in terms of:

- **technology,** e.g. trends towards innovations, new technologies or combinations of existing technologies

- **society**, e.g. societal trends, emerging structures, conflicts

- **economics**, e.g. the most likely impacts of raw material costs; supply and demand for basics such as energy, water, food; interest and exchange rates; labour markets and growth rates.

The teams then create scenarios (stories, if you will) and test these against the forecasts to see which scenarios are more likely to survive under which sets of conditions. The strength of Scenario Building is that it accepts that, in a chaotic world, pinpoint forecasting has been shown to be an inaccurate and therefore unhelpful approach. However, more flexible clusters of tendencies can be assembled and their robustness tested against measures such as numerically based trends. If the scenarios are convincing enough to attract the attention of the Board of Directors, they can be converted into strategy statements. Multi-location or multi-national organisations may prefer to publish centrally derived scenarios and assumptions and allow local companies to fine-tune their own versions. This approach allows big organisations to think centrally but to act in a more flexible and dispersed manner.

Although scenarios are often thought of as requiring sophisticated inputs, it is quite possible for small to medium sized organisations or a school or parish council to produce worthwhile results by following the instructions below. At its simplest, the technique is a structured way of requiring participants to imagine living through a number of future possibilities and deciding what opportunities and threats the future may hold. It is somewhat like performing a SWOT exercise (**S**trengths, **W**eaknesses, **O**pportunities and **T**hreats).

How to operate the tool 'Scenario Building' with a small group
It should be explained to the group that pinpoint forecasting simply does not work well enough and therefore your group has to find another basis for its planning. One of the outcomes of applying this tool is that the participants will appreciate the range of future uncertainties and hopefully will see that this has positive as well as negative consequences. Not only does the creation of a range of possible 'futures' highlight potential difficulties, it also indicates possible benefits. By working with these factors the group starts to

live the future to some extent.

This future search tool also helps you to focus on 'weak signals' coming from your environment. For example, Britain's once-thriving cotton industry could have picked up signals that the Far Eastern operatives (who also grow the cotton) were likely to vertically integrate their activities and usurp Britain's manufacturing position. The even lower wages in the Far East and ready access to the raw supplies meant that all the economic indicators were in their favour. All the signals were there, but the cotton supremos in the North of England did not pick them up.

A very similar story applies to the American railway systems when, in the late 19th and early 20th centuries, they failed to spot the ascendancy of motor transport. Another example of failure to pick up weak signals can be seen in the film, *A Bridge Too Far*, about Montgomery's plan 'market garden' to leapfrog over the retreating Germans, capture three Rhine bridges and get to Berlin by Christmas. 16,000 aerial reconnaissance photographs had been taken over the Allied routes but only the last three (very weak signals) showed Panzer tanks at Arnhem.

Senior managers can behave like generals when the plans have been made and they are raring to go. Tools like scenarios, cognitive mapping and, especially, systems dynamics can sometimes help them to see the folly of continuing into the equivalent of a death-trap. Similarly, NASA's determination to launch Challenger, despite warnings from scientists about their lack of readiness, led to the well-known disaster and the loss of astronauts' lives.

Step 1

Agree the time frame for the exercise – 2010 is suggested. Thinking about 2010 – what is certain? What is uncertain? What is highly relevant for your organisation? What is less relevant? Write these ideas briefly on post-its and place these on a flip chart(s) which has the vertical axis –'Uncertainty' (from low to high) and the horizontal axis –'Importance' (from low to high). After completing this step, there should be about five post-its on the right hand edge of your chart that will be called the key variables (because they are 'important') and will be used later in the process. Do not throw away or not put

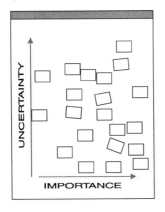

forward any wild post-its; they are all valid ideas, i.e. divergent thinking is required.

Step 2

Each participant must now **invent two or three stories** as a series of events that take place from now until 2010 – you can think of these as a series of newspaper headlines, i.e. keep them brief. Examples could be 'Only hydrogen fuel allowed', 'Brain transplant patient meets King', 'Muslims take over', 'China takes over'. Write up each event (i.e. each step in your story) on a separate post-it. Put the post-its on a wall or chart in time order and explain the logic to your colleagues. The stories show only what might happen but must be of relevance (not what should happen or necessarily will happen). Each story should cover one or more of the key variables identified in step 1. The group should then prune and merge the post-it stories, asking each other whether the resultant combined story lines are:

- plausible rather than fanciful
- recognisable, rather than alien
- challenging, rather than boring
- important, rather than irrelevant.

The result should be two to four rich post-it story-lines, either with some common steps or completely independent, or even with branching points somewhere down the time path. These branches indicate that the story could develop in a number of different ways.

Step 3

Go back to the key variables identified in step 1 and talk through no more than five of these. Write onto the flip chart grid what happens to each variable in each story.

If any embryonic scenarios do not make any difference to the overall (key) variables, then drop them.

Finally, with only two or three scenarios left, give each a short but distinctive name. Summarise the total scenario by stating the name, the key features and if relevant what makes any branch occur.

Step 4

Draw a grid and mark on these two opportunities and two threats for each scenario. Consider these in terms of factors that are important for your group, maybe social unrest or world peace or market volatility or competence requirements. Deciding what to do about the opportunities and threats becomes your strategy.

Other big tools

Three of the other potentially big tools used either for solving large socio-technical issues and/or scanning the future for opportunities and threats are:

- Systems dynamics and planning
- Kepner-Tregoe
- Cognitive mapping.

These tools – elaborated below – have been classified as 'big' because they require specialist facilitation and would engage a group of managers to input their knowledge of the organisation over about a day – possibly less in the case of Kepner-Tregoe. Every large organisation should have a facilitator who can lead groups through the first two of these or at least know how they can obtain such advice. Managers need not know *how* to apply the tools, but they should know what sorts of issues *can be resolved* by applying them.

Systems dynamics

As a tool, it surfaces the assumptions that the participants are making about the current and future workings of the group and of any impact from their environment. This can lead to conflict about what differing individuals think is important; however working through this conflict has led some organisations to say the process was worthwhile simply for that cathartic experience – even regardless of the other benefits. It also produces a road map of the future and allows an organisation to perform 'what-if' experiments with the future. In this mode, the tool has been called a management flight simulator – better to crash in a simulation model than after investing millions into a new product or plant. It also shows that quite small interventions can yield very high leverage on future results – which has to be every manager's dream. For example, it is well known that an oil tanker has so much momentum that it is very difficult to turn quickly at sea. However, a small secondary rudder (known as a trimtap) attached to the main rudder can increase the turning capacity of the ship by 40%.

The approach also enables one to see the inter-relationships between different (perhaps remote) parts of the system and should also enable the spotting of trends in their early stages. This is the same concept as using 'scenarios' to spot weak signals as mentioned above. The power of exponential growth (e.g. that of the internet or of e-commerce) means that if only you can detect the early weak signs of growth, you can prepare your organisation before it is overwhelmed. Another powerful result of applying a systems approach is that often the dynamic complexity of the organisation or trend is significantly *less* than the complexity of the detail. Thus if you understand some key aspects about *how* a system operates, you do not have to deal with all the details because you will be able to forecast the outcome of almost any set of changes. After participants have given their assumptions and judgements about how the organisation works, these can be converted into measures of stocks and flows to enable predictive numerical models to be constructed. It is these models that can be used to test the various what-if possibilities and test alternative futures. Readers who know something of electronics or control theory will recognise some of the origins of systems dynamics – involving the interaction of exponential growth or decay with damping effects. To discover more about systems dynamics read *The Fifth Discipline Fieldbook* by P. Senge et al or contact London Business School, who run workshops.

Kepner-Tregoe

The Kepner-Tregoe approach has been described briefly in chapter 2. Those wishing to understand if it might have applications to their work should read *The New Rational Manager* by Messrs Kepner and

Tregoe, published by Princeton Research Press or attend one of the workshops organised by the British subsidiary.

Cognitive mapping

This is perhaps the most specialist of the tools mentioned here. It requires expert facilitation such as that provided by some of the staff at Strathclyde University, e.g. Professor Colin Eden et al. Somewhat akin to systems dynamics the facilitator will engage a group of managers and ask carefully prepared questions about which aspects of the organisation seem to them to have a key influence on other parts of the organisation. Software called COPE can analyse their responses and gradually build a causal map of the organisation. The map consists of certain nodes (e.g. the organisation's reputation) and causal arrows will link the nodes. Inspection of the map will enable one to identify the critical nodes and to decide which courses of action might strengthen or weaken that node. Thus, in times of crisis – such as some major organisational change, a take-over battle, divesting or contemplating a joint venture – one can see what might help and what might hinder the preferred direction of change. Because big system or organisational change can be rather complex, there can be counter-intuitive effects. For example, a decision to bomb another country into submission may not work if a key factor is the enemy's spirit, such that bombing can be less effective than other measures and even lengthen the outcome of the hostility. Shooting a troublesome guerrilla leader, whilst quick and decisive, is also irreversible and might grant him martyr status, thus lengthening the problem. An advantage of cognitive mapping is that one outcome is a database of connecting elements that can be interrogated via any of the variables, thus producing analyses from different perspectives.

Classifications of tools: how to select the best tool for the job

The ease-value matrix (see figure 27) shows a range of tools according to their ease of application and their overall value. The names of the tools themselves and the types of techniques are drawn from the book by J. Martin, 'Innovation and change', Techniques

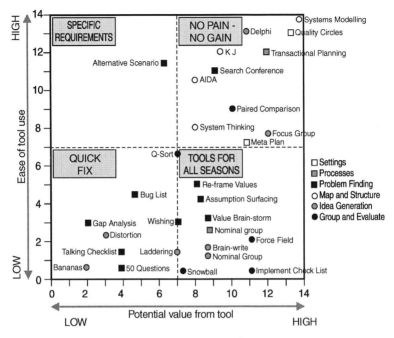

Figure 27 – The ease/value matrix

library, OU press, and from the OU's B822 course on creative management.

One of the commonest questions heard in tool selection is how to resolve the dilemma of '... will it do the job well *versus* how much effort will I/we have to input to apply the tool?'

This effort comprises several factors.

● Learning how to apply the tool, especially if it is new to you. Some of the biggest tools, e.g. Kepner-Tregoe or Systems Dynamics can take a week or longer to master.

● Does it require an expert facilitator? This is one way to reduce the time taken to use the tool, albeit at a price.

● Does it require equipment, e.g IT applications?

By contrast, many of the tools described in this book are small enough and intuitive enough to be learned and applied within 15 minutes. The

123

dilemma of trading off 'effort required' against 'ease of use' can be reduced by consulting the 'ease-value' matrix – see figure 27. Note that some of the tools lie nearer the top right-hand corner of the matrix – i.e. they offer relatively more value per unit of effort than the tools nearer to the bottom left. Tools in the lower, right-hand window have been labelled '**Tools for all seasons**'. The other three windows of the matrix have been labelled as follows:

- **Quick fix** – These are the small scope tools that are easiest to learn and apply. Do not expect serious break-through outcomes but correspondingly don't write them off; they are not trivial and can lead to significant insights. They may be of particular interest to facilitators who know several of them by heart and can employ them to move a stuck group.

- **Specific requirements** – Only one tool is shown in this window because they are relatively rare. They are also not so widely known because they are so specific and require more than the usual amount of effort to employ. You may need the assistance of a facilitator who has previously applied the tools.

- **No pain – no gain** – These tools are located past the half-way diagonal, i.e. they are bigger tools, thus requiring more resources (time, external facilitators, computer aided, access to expert views). However, when applied to an appropriate 'big' and/or expensive problem, they will yield high quality results.

Approaches to the implementation of ideas or solutions

This final phase of problem solving has borrowed many concepts from the arenas of both the management of change and project management. If the group who defined the problem and worked on the possible solutions is also to be involved in the implementation, then it is vital to increase their ownership of the outcomes. Full involvement through the above processes will help to make them feel like the problem owners.

One of the significant advantages of the meta-plan approach to group problem solving (see chapter 7) is that, in the final step, there is an opportunity for participants to choose which issue or aspect of the (bigger) issue they wish to bring to fruition. Meta-plan involves the use of post-its or similar materials so that the various stages of the problem solving are made very visible and can readily be changed and/or added to. In the final stages of the process, there are typically aspects of the bigger problem broken into components represented by clusters of post-its. At this stage members of the group can be asked to choose which cluster they volunteer to implement – they should be encouraged to take the cluster of concepts with them. They should also be required to commit in public to a date by which they will have completed the final steps. It is important to achieve this assignment stage before the group leave the room and disperse. Trying to re-engage the group at a later stage can be very difficult.

The idea generation stage (step 3 of the 4-diamond model) and the implementation or innovation stage (step 4) are usually seen as requiring skills and motivations that are so different as to be almost mutually exclusive. The imaginative types who enjoy idea generation frequently do not excel at the hard slog of implementation. In Kirton terms, the former have a preference for the 'innovator' style while the latter prefer and therefore more frequently adopt the 'adaptive' approach. Clearly both styles can manage both sets of tasks if they are sufficiently motivated to do so.

However, if stress levels are raised – for example by tight time pressures to complete the tasks or from interference from other jobs – then the outcome may suffer. Some organisations go as far as assigning different types of people to the different stages of problem solving but this has the disadvantage of managing the hand over. It may be sufficient for the individuals simply to know about their preferred styles and the consequences – this should enable them to compensate. Alternatively a pairing of adaptors with innovators will help.

Those who are embarking on the implementation stage should remember that they will need:

- a clear vision of what they are trying to achieve and this vision should be as motivating as possible

- a plan of the first practical steps

- support from the senior parts of the organisation (e.g. from a new product champion or perhaps from the problem owner)

- to have considered the riskiest parts of the implementation and have built a contingency plan for these risks

- a set of milestones and possibly a method of measuring progress.

Some options for the question about football on page 107.

1. Change the aerodynamics of the ball. This was done during the 2000 World Cup. There was also a Brit who, in 1994, tested 30 different materials/coatings for football boots that would help the kicker to impart so much spin that the ball would swerve quite violently through the air.

2. Give the referees and linesmen more (electronic) aids. Already there are radio links between the officials. However, it would be easy and cheap to lay conducting cables under the pitch that could produce off-side decisions with millimetre precision. The cables would also warm the pitch to melt ice and snow. There are already shirts containing miniature strain gauges that would alert officials to shirt tugging.

3. Change the stadium, e.g. for multiple usage. In Eindhoven in the Netherlands, the pitch can be rolled off to convert the space to a swimming pool or a dance/meeting space. This could reduced the cost of attendance.

4. Hand-held instant replay video recorders would enable rapid and quality decisions from the officials.

5. Professor de Bruyn from Antwerp University suggests that changing the pitch layout would produce different versions of the game. One version has the two goals on adjacent sides of a square.

6. We already have 'football' played from wheel-chairs and bicycles - what other extensions can you imagine?

7. Think of a change to the existing rules.

8. Gender changes - there have been a (very) few female referees - it seems that the (male) players do not like them very much. Some leagues require that at least three women are on the field at any one time.

9. The de-regulation of football has seen many more nations playing across national boundaries. Try force-fitting the deregulation of trains and buses to football.

8

The Competences of Creative Problem Solving and How to Improve Them

'Our life is what our thoughts make it.'
Marcus Aurelius

'Everything has changed except our way of thinking.'
Albert Einstein

Any improvement system needs a target. It is helpful if this target contains numerical measures because it is then easier to measure performance towards the target. For example a target statement such as '25% of sales to be based on products developed over the last 3 years' is better than 'I promise myself to make less mistakes this year'. The so-called 'stretch' targets are popular in the new millennium since they force participants to take them more seriously and they may be more motivational. There is research that shows that participants who were set say an 85% target may well achieve 60%; however others who were set a 110% target achieved 70% – it indeed seems to be a matter that setting one's sights higher actually produces better results.

However, it is accepted that for some areas such as artistic creativity, it will be difficult to produce such concrete objectives.

A typical competence improvement process will have the following 7 steps:

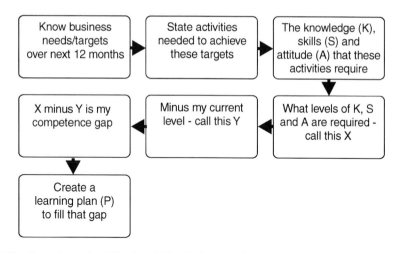

The learning plan (P) should include a variety of different methods of learning. Accordingly, it should not just rely on, say, reading as a method of gathering competence. Ideally the plan would also contain ideas for doing something (e.g. facilitating a group through a problem solving process or realising an opportunity into some concrete advantage) and obtaining feedback on that activity. Another type of activity would be to complete a questionnaire which measures your problem solving style, such as the Kirton instrument and to discuss and verify the results with at least one other person who knows you well. You should then address the question 'so what?' and make a list of the consequences – both positive and negative – of having the particular style indicated by the results of the questionnaire.

Yet another part of the plan could be to make contact with some external organisation such as the European Association of Creativity and Innovation (**www.eaci.net / eaci@eaci.net**) or the Creativity Institute at Buffalo and see specifically what they have to offer that would fit some of your knowledge or skills gaps.

There are many advantages to be gained from applying the above 7-step process to yourself and/or your work group. To ensure that the first step (targets) is well linked to your business needs or organisation's objectives, you may well need to speak to your boss and/or obtain access to business plans. The above 7-step process may seem rather complicated, because you create your own list from a blank sheet of paper. However, because it has been focussed specifically on your needs or those of your group, it will be much more relevant and therefore more reliable than a simpler 'off the shelf' approach – such as that described below. The competences of creative problem solving itself can also be derived from the list.

Figure 28 – The competences of creative problem solving for those wanting an 'off the shelf' solution.

Note that although quicker than working rigorously from your actual situation, it may not be as effective.

Aspect	Examples/comments
Divergent thinking needs:	
a) imagination	able to reframe and see issues from different perspectives
b) intuition	see section below on intuition
c) risk taking	does not mean being blind to risks; for serious consequences, ensure you have a contingency plan
d) desire to solve problems for their own sake	being open to new experiences; this is hard to train for improvement and under stress one may well revert to preferred approach
e) ambiguity tolerance	as above, this is another deep-rooted part of personality and as such not easy to train for
f) challenging the status quo	not to be a destructive criticism; must aim at adding value to the challenged concept
Convergent thinking needs:	
a) being realistic with choices	know tools for improving ideas, e.g. the 'C' box
Overall process needs:	
a) ability to apply tools for all 4 diamonds	know where to find details of other tools if initial choice does not work well

b) ability to facilitate others — know how to cope with 'blocks' to creativity; know a step-by-step process for facilitating

c) as well as planning to build on strengths, it may also be necessary to have a plan for identifying and diminishing weaknesses. These may well be deeply ingrained parts of one's character, painful to face up to and difficult to deal with. Examples could be:

- excessive conformity (e.g. needing a lot of approval from others or not being able to cope realistically with hostility from a group)

- being overly defensive when one's ideas are ignored or attacked

- being obsessive perhaps over details and not being able to see the bigger picture.

Rather than having to face up to issues like these in public, it may be more helpful to take one of the self-administered questionnaires mentioned in chapter 3. The better versions contain both 'norm' data – i.e. you can see where your score or result fits in relationship to others, and some ideas on what to do about your result.

Competences of innovation (implementing ideas)

Persistence – above all else you will certainly need a lot of self-motivated drive. It is therefore often useful to have mapped out your support network that will enable you to contact others with specific expertise such as marketing, or contacting venture capitalists for financing. You will also need some political skills; introverts sometimes find these harder to implement than extroverts. If you think that the world is not treating your invention fairly, try reading *Against the Odds* by James Dyson (see chapter 9) and you should be able to put your problems into perspective.

You will also need the following skills:

- **managing change** – there are some fairly simple basic tips such as having as clear a vision as you can of what you want; having a plan for the first few steps and having some support – the more powerful the better.

- **influencing skills** – these may also be called negotiating, selling, or marketing skills. Often a first step is to be aware of your own preferred style of influencing and guess the preferred style of your target –it may not be the same as yours. For example, technically trained people may rely excessively on logic. On the other hand their audience may just want to know about the costs or some of the benefits of the new item.

From the lists in figure 28, you can quickly choose up to say three aspects where you could do better and that you will need in the next 12 months. As with the more rigorous 7-step approach, the next step is to make a learning plan for remedying these deficiencies. Another checklist approach to improving your creative problem solving is to examine the list of 'thunks' that are quoted in *Conceptual Toolmaking*, by J D Rhodes, published by Blackwell. Thunks are the basic building blocks of effective thinking in Rhodes' approach to creative problem solving.

Competences can be thought of as the interweaving of the knowledge, skills and attitude to complete a particular set of tasks. In order to maintain simplicity, figure 28 identified only those immediately involved in divergence/convergence/process and implementation. For those who wish to go further, the knowledge and skills requirements defined below will give a more sophisticated guide. The examples given below have assumed that you are solving problems alone or in a pair, or a trio. If in fact you are leading a group of colleagues, you should also look at the competences involved in facilitating a group.

Knowledge of creative problem solving
You should aim beyond simply being able to repeat a description or definition after having read it. Effective use of 'knowledge' means that you can apply the facts/model to various situations.

- Immerse yourself in the details and history of your target area. Know what has been tried, what failed and if possible some ideas on why it failed.

- Know and be able to apply all the steps of the 4-diamond model. Know under what conditions one can run the first two diamonds together and under which situations this should definitely not be done.

- Know and be able to apply at least one tool for each of the four diamonds.

Other skills of creative problem solving

Skills of insight

- ability to learn from ongoing applications
- ability to learn from mistakes
- ability to reframe problem statements in an imaginative and motivating way and with realistic concepts

Skills of imagination

- ability to view a problem from different perspectives
- ability to visualise a problem – this could well be achieved by having completed three visualisation exercises (see the end of this chapter).

Skills of intuition

Intuition – sometimes called the sixth sense – has been defined in quite different ways, for example the Myers-Briggs definition is relatively concrete ('a way of acquiring information') and can be measured, whereas others view it as a spiritual matter, for example defining it as 'direct knowing'. Webster's dictionary defines it as 'the power of knowing, or knowledge obtained without recourse to inference or reasoning; innate or instinctive knowledge; familiarly, a quick or ready apprehension'. Carl Jung (whose work lead to the Myers-Briggs approach) wrote that intuition 'does not denote something contrary to reason, but something outside the province of reason'.

Intuition is therefore quite an elusive concept and it could be argued that the statements involved below are not skills but examples of the 'attitude' dimension of competence: -

- Ability to trust your inner voice, even when under considerable confrontation from others – even those in power positions over you.

- Ability to be realistic in terms of what self censoring of ideas one does.

- Have measured and understood one's 'intuition' score from the Myers-Briggs indicator.

- Ability to recognise and compensate for other preferences that one has in different circumstances that interfere with one's intuition.

To explore and hopefully improve your intuition, the following resources are recommended.

📖 The book *Intuition: the New Frontier of Management* by J. Parikh and F. Neubauer, published by Blackwell. This contains many models of the components of intuition and the results of a multi-national survey conducted by the authors at the Swiss business school in Lausanne – IMD.

📖 The book *The Intuitive Edge* by Philip Goldberg published by Tarcher in 1983 and by Touchstone.

🎧 There is also a 60 minute audio tape *To Unlock Your Intuition* by Goldberg, produced by Audio Renaissance Tapes, Los Angeles. The tape investigates what intuition is and what it is not by examining six types of intuition. It also contains various exercises to develop your own intuition.

🎧 Willis Harman has produced a 60 minute audio tape called *Create Your Future.*

📖 Willis Harman's book *Higher Creativity* is strongly recommended. These and a wide range of similar material is marketed by the Noetic Science Foundation, 475 Gate Five Road, Suite 300, Sausalito, 94965-0909, near San Fransisco, US telephone (area code(415) 331-5650.

Towards the end of his active career, Willis Harman was the president of the Institute for Noetic Sciences and may appeal to those trained in technical and scientific disciplines. He gained a PhD in electrical engineering from Stanford University where he later became Professor of Engineering-Economic systems and was also a member of the Board of Regents of the University of California. The Noetic

Science Institute itself was founded in 1973 by Edgar Mitchell who was the astronaut who had a profound (spiritual) experience while travelling to the moon. Noetics is the study of different ways of knowing or understanding. The Institute is a non-profit organisation that networks world-class scientists and scholars and publishes the results of studies aimed at expanding the knowledge and potential of the mind. For example, they have published well-regarded studies about options for the future of our planet (health, safety and environmental aspects); about expanding the foundations of science; about the role of business and about psychoneuroimmunology – examining the systems of linkage between the brain, mind and the immune systems.

Spirituality in creative problem solving
Figure 28 depicts a graduated staircase of spirituality. Case-hardened technicians and scientists may prefer to leave the staircase early along the curve only accepting the utility of dreams, bio-feedback, hypnosis and perhaps the use of meditation as reasonably proven phenomena. Others may be happy to accept the entire spectrum and perhaps even beyond the steps shown.

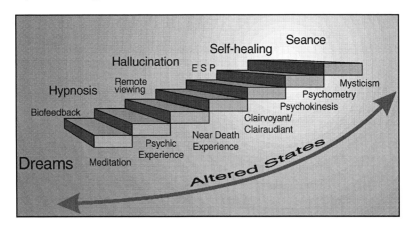

Figure 29 – Staircase of spirituality

📖 Diary time

Exercise   1. To explore your own relationship to the staircase try to discover your own intuition. If you can obtain the Myers-Briggs questionnaire (see chapter 2 for an explanation),this is a good starting point for measuring your intuition. Some of the books and tapes mentioned above should also help you to develop your intuitive powers.

2. If you are not comfortable with any of the steps on the staircase – ask yourself why not? Were there some events which put you off such matters or do you share some views with a parent or close friend?

'Attitude' component of the competences of creative problem solving and innovation

The following components are needed:

- persistence and a disposition that usually is optimistic – thus being able to cope with getting stuck at the micro level and at the macro level, possibly having your invention rejected for the 99th time

- coping with situations in groups where the process is not going well and especially if the other group members are looking to you for results

- the genuine and unforced quality of being non-judgemental during periods of divergent thinking – especially with respect to the ideas of others

- the preparedness to help others improve their ideas and/or see them from a different perspective.

Levels of competence

Identifying the area of competence that you need to improve is only part of the issue, since you should also decide the level that you need to reach. For example, it would not be a very wise strategy to invest a lot of effort to become world class in an aspect that you only needed to use once a year. It may be obvious to you what you need to improve upon in order to satisfy the demands placed upon you in the 'area' of creativity and innovation. However, if it becomes a key part of an important project or if you are responsible for the competence of others, then you may find the following definitions of levels of competence helpful.

Level 1 – sound understanding – A good knowledge of what is involved in the area and its relevance to your work. You will be able to describe the main elements within the area and their importance to you/your work.

Level 2 – working knowledge – Being able to interpret and evaluate information and advice from experts in the area. You will be able to remember and use correctly the terminology; to hold an informed debate with experts and ask questions that test the viability of any proposals.

Level 3 – can do – Being able to carry out consistently the activities within the area to the required standard. You will be able to perform satisfactorily the majority of activities within the area and be able to translate guidelines into practical actions. You will also be able to guide and advise others (see chapter 9 about facilitating groups through problem solving).

Level 4 – trouble shoot/adapt – Being able to diagnose and resolve unusual problems and to successfully adapt aspects of the area. You will be able to creatively solve significant, complex, non-routine problems and adapt practices from other sources.

Level 5 – develop new – Being able to develop significant and new approaches or methods within the area. You will be able to develop new approaches and novel applications.

More about the brain and its impact on creativity

In a brain map of what is involved in 'creativity', it is through the branches labelled for intuition and 'p for person' that the spiritual aspects crop up most frequently. So much of the so-called evidence is very hard to verify or even to obtain for oneself and readers are right to be wary. For example, there are many claims for remote viewing as manifestations of extra sensory perception (ESP). Examples are usually of two persons who are carefully separated and cannot communicate by classical means. The transmitting person then places, say, a drawing in an envelope that is given to a trusted third party; both the transmitter and the receiving person then concentrate on sending and receiving an image of the drawing. The receiver draws an image of what he or she saw in the mind's eye, which is then compared with the image drawn by the transmitter before the experiment. However, the author does not know of any cases that have been scrutinised by careful means, by independent observers of probity.

There is also a claim that young children have interesting powers of 'second sight'. Between 1927 and 1967, experiments were conducted into ESP at Duke University in North Carolina. The leaders of the research teams were Dr JB and Louisa Rhine. The author has visited the University and although the visit was for only one day, the controls and care that had been taken with the experiments was impressive. The experiments used the now famous Duke cards (also called Zener cards) developed at the Durham campus of Duke University. The cards are approximately the same size as playing cards and carry quite distinct symbols, e.g. a star, a circle, a square, a cross and wavy lines. Similar to the remote viewing cases described above, the Duke experiments involved people who acted as a transmitter and a receiver who were isolated by various means. The isolation consisted of combinations of physical and geographic separation and isolation from electro-magnetic links such as radio by placing the subjects in a metal cage with or without a surrounding shield of an electric or magnetic field.

By using sufficient numbers of the Duke cards carrying say five of the symbols, then if there is no ESP effect, then 1 in 5 or 20% of the symbols will be guessed correctly but purely randomly by chance. Scores above 20%, especially if they can be repeated, become interesting. The overwhelming majority of subjects showed no special ability to either transmit or to receive. But some few people did and in particular young children aged about three tested positive, although this ability reduced drastically with age. At age three, an amazing 46% was recorded; over twice the expected value – but by age five the subjects' scores were back to 26 %. It was hypothesised that the increased fluency and growth of language centres in the brain was driving out this other telepathic capacity. Although we understand an enormous amount more of the brain than we did in the 1940s, it is probably best to put these strange effects in the 'not yet explainable' tray. After all, it used to be a mystery as to how birds such as pigeons could migrate so accurately – now it known that they have small amounts of iron-containing compounds in their brains and the hypothesis is that this acts in concert with the earth's magnetic field such that they have a version of an auto-pilot. In his book *The Emperor's New Mind*, Professor Roger Penrose describes the strange phenomena known as 'backward chaining' in which a muscle acts as if it had received signals via the brain before these signals had been activated. This definitely needs to go into the 'not yet explainable' category, albeit that physicists are currently drawing on quantum mechanical effects to try to explain how the brain completes some data transfers so quickly.

There are also well documented cases of people with photographic memories or the capacity to draw complex images (such as the Houses of Parliament) from memory. If you want to read more about the brain and in particular some of its malfunctions that inform us so much about its operations, the following are suggested:

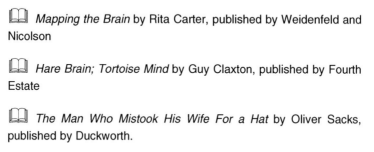

📖 *Mapping the Brain* by Rita Carter, published by Weidenfeld and Nicolson

📖 *Hare Brain; Tortoise Mind* by Guy Claxton, published by Fourth Estate

📖 *The Man Who Mistook His Wife For a Hat* by Oliver Sacks, published by Duckworth.

However, it is now clear to the author that the brain can affect the body and that various parts of the brain can influence other parts – whether it helps to label these parts as the conscious and the subconscious does not seem to add value to the debate. There does seem to be more believable evidence for auto-suggestion – such that belief can produce physical effects – both positive and negative. On the positive side, examples can be found where patients, for example cancer sufferers, can become better or achieve some sort of remission by concentrating on positive messages. In one form of this therapy, the sufferers are taught how to visualise their white cells as the good guys and how to will them to succeed. There was an interesting experiment carried out on the post-operative healing of three groups of patients in Israel. One group was the control and nothing special was done for them; a second group was told that the very best medical treatment was available for them. The third group was told that special prayers for their recovery were being made. The three groups were all large enough for the results to have statistical validity and the groups were carefully chosen to be equivalent samples, i.e. they were mixed to contain equal numbers of the same types of operations. They were also carefully matched by gender and age. The third group that believed they were being prayed for recovered best and the differences from the other groups were statistically significant, i.e. did not occur purely by chance.

The negative side of auto-suggestion are the voodoo and related cults that claim to be able to cause illness or death even at a distance – the victim simply has to believe that the threat is real. Certainly altered brain states explain some bizarre situations that not long ago would have been filed under magic. Fakirs who can cope with great pain (the bed of nails) can also change some of their body functions – for example lowering respiration rates so that they can survive being buried alive. They would appear to be using some sort of self-hypnosis and accessing a brain-state akin to that of a trance.

The hypnotic state imposed by a third party can also produce the most bizarre effects. Anyone who has seen a friend respond to the effects of a post-hypnotic signal will testify to the reality of the behaviour. For example, under hypnosis, a subject is told that when they hear a clock strike a certain time, they will imitate a chicken or that on drinking some non-alcoholic drink they will become quite inebriated.

The author has known several senior managers who relied on their own senses of intuition (the sixth sense) to solve problems or to make educated guesses about the future. Even Einstein who to many appears to be a very scientific and technical figure, said that 'imagination is more important than knowledge' and in practice he used a combination of reason and intuition.

Visualisation exercises

These exercises examine your imagination and, if performed in a group, allow you to compare your imagination with those of others. Before each exercise, ensure that you are relaxed by either lying down or sitting comfortably. If sitting, do not cross your legs, and allow your arms either to hang loosely by your side or cup one hand in the other on your lap. Try to minimise any external noises such as traffic or radio and now – perhaps with eyes closed – start to relax. Firstly, increase the depth of your breathing – draw in deep breaths, hold them for a second and then slowly let them escape. If you are still working through events of the day or some annoyance in your mind, then imagine bubbles of breath entering your lungs and working their way around your body – allow the bubbles to change colour, gradually changing into a deeply relaxing yellow hue. Imagine that they absorb the troubles of the day and sweep them from your body as you exhale.

Note that participants can move into an almost trance-like state and may be difficult to rouse at the end of the exercise. It is suggested that they are not woken up suddenly, but that the exercise comes to a planned ending – such as 'as you come out of the wood, cross the ten stones and return to the room; cross the stones – nine, eight, seven, ... one'. It is also possible that deep visualisation may stir up unpleasant memories. If you have any reason to expect this, do not use the exercise.

Exercise 1
After relaxing, try to imagine a cow. Slowly encourage the cow to walk and then gradually to run faster and faster. Now start to morph the cow into a race horse and allow it to canter at full speed. Finally either bring the horse to a slower trot and then to stop or morph it back into a cow and bring that to a halt. Most people can manage this exercise quite easily, but some have a much richer experience. For example what were the colours of the cow and horse – were they similar or quite different? Did you hear or smell the animals?

Exercise 2

Imagine that you are going on a walk on a lovely warm day. Feel the warmth of the sun on your shoulders and arms. As you start down the path, you notice some attractive flowers – go over to them and smell and enjoy their fragrance. Rejoin the path and enter a small wood. You pause by some trees and feel the bark for a few seconds. Continuing on the path, you wonder at the loveliness of the day and your own happiness. Pause and listen to the birds singing in the trees. Through the trees you see some water and decide to go over to it and stay for a while. Continuing along the path you see a building in front of you – go up to it and look through the windows. You decide to go inside and explore. On leaving the building you rejoin the path but feel that you are being watched – you look back and see someone standing in the doorway. They have something in their hand and seem to be offering it to you. Go back, gratefully accept it and then continue the walk. The path starts to climb upwards and after quite a stiff climb you find yourself on the top of a small hill – you admire the view and retrace your steps back down hill. You see some stepping stones in front of you and realise that the walk will be over when you reach the end of the stones. You cross the stones, ten, nine … three, two, one.

Now wiggle your toes, roll your shoulders and in your own time come back into the room.

Clearly this exercise allows you to examine all your senses of imagination – smell, sound, texture etc. People often vary in the quality of being able to conjure up these different senses – which worked most vividly for you? The wording of the exercise is deliberately vague to allow participants to produce their own imaginations. Was the water a placid lake or a turbulent rushing stream? Did you return to known places or childhood reminiscences for some of the images? What was the present from the person at the building – did you know the person? Climbing the hill is said to bring out peak or good memories and other versions of the visualisation go down into a cave which seems to bring out negative events. One version (not recommended) even takes you to the cliff edge above a very steep gorge and requires you to jump off!

Exercise 3

After relaxing, realise that you are looking at the photograph of someone that you know. Focus carefully on the picture and try to imagine that person as a lot younger or older than they appear in the photo. Then mentally return their image to the way you found it. Many people take the easy route and choose a photo of someone they actually have seen as an older or younger person. If they have not, it can be the hardest of the three exercises since you are trying to imagine something that you have never seen.

Other visualisations are available on audio tape – one of the author's favourites takes you up in the air until you can see the earth below you as that wonderful green, white and blue image captured in the space programme. You then drift off into the galaxy! These exercises nearly always produce a deep sense of relaxation and are generally regarded as good fun – the business needs they serve are rather dubious, except allowing participants to check out their sense of imagination against those of their colleagues. Clearly a good sense of imagination is helpful in visioning a novel invention. The oil company Texaco has used the technique to enable its reservoir engineers and production technologists to walk through hydrocarbon reservoirs to see how they might flush out the oil and gas lying trapped in the rock.

Playing music usually heightens the vividness of the images and workers at Antwerp University have employed this to help participants to conjure up solutions to problems. Imagine for example that you are a traffic engineer earning your living solving city centre congestion. After relaxing, you focus on the most congested city you know. Melodious music may next be used to flush out random thoughts, then maybe an excerpt from Kraftwerk which sounds just like heavy traffic. This does not produce novel solutions because it simply provokes a left-brain, analytical solution, often a known solution. Various passages of very different types of music may conjure more novel possibilities. It seems that 3-dimensional music – i.e. with a wide range of frequencies produces 3-dimensional solutions such as fly-overs or the use of air-ships instead of cars. The resultant images are usually not working solutions – they may even be intermediate impossibles – and will need coaxing into sensible proposals. Perfumes and other smells have also been used to stimulate the imagination but do not work so well. The nose communicates over a short distance and direct into the brain and seems to evoke memories rather than novel images. These memories could be used to stimulate thinking, but the entire process does not work so effectively.

9

Facilitating Creative Problem Solving

'You are wrong and I am right.'
Book by Edward de Bono

*'Our task is to make the familiar strange
and the strange familiar.'*
Anonymous facilitator

*'Great strategies like great works of art or great scientific
discoveries call for technical mastery but originate in insights
that are beyond the reach of conscious analysis.'*
K Ohmae in *The mind of the Strategist*

📖 Diary time

Exercise   Have you ever facilitated a group through any sort
of process – whether it was planning this year's
garden fete or this year's budget or strategy
formulation?

If yes, please make some notes about which
aspects went well for you (e.g. maybe you prepared
very carefully, maybe the group was supportive,
maybe you had a friend in the group with whom
you'd had a prior chat or maybe you had received
prior training).

Please also make some notes about aspects that did not go so well and what you learned from that. Did you seek feedback from the audience? Some people find this difficult to do, especially if they have some doubts about the quality of their performance; however, it is a very powerful way to learn how to improve. As it says in the Torah, if one man tells you you are an ass you can ignore him; but if three men tell you the same – then go and buy yourself a saddle.

If you have never facilitated a group

There is in fact no need to facilitate others if you simply wish to improve your own problem-solving abilities. However, if you are a supervisor/manager/teacher or some other type of leader, you will probably want to apply some of the concepts below. Practice is the key to successful facilitation, but try very hard to arrange that your first attempt is a success. It will also help enormously if you have already been accepted in the role of facilitator, otherwise the group may resent your taking their time and imposing yourself upon them. Unless you are planning something very basic (like simply suggesting that the group tries a brainstorm), then set some expectations for the group as to how long your intervention will take and a quick outline of what will be involved. If you have some friends in the group, it may be worth briefing them before the event and gaining their support. If it is both one of your first attempts at group facilitation and if the group is new to problem solving processes, then events will probably take longer than you might expect.

Remember both to ask for questions and allow time for responses. For your first or second run, it is strongly suggested that you keep things simple. Do not fall into the trap of wanting to show off your new knowledge by complicating things. If you are still somewhat unsure about taking on the facilitator's role in front of a group of your colleagues, consider finding some other venue for your debut with strangers that you will never have to meet again. Alternatively persuade a more experienced facilitator to allow you to co-facilitate with them a few times before your fly solo.

Facilitating style

From chapter 3, you will have understood that people vary in their styles of doing things and this applies as much to facilitation styles as to anything else. Try to form a view of what your style is like and how this might compliment or clash with members of your audience. For example, are you keen or even over-keen on detailed explanations or do you feel you prefer a broad-brush approach? Do you have a habit of displaying your expertise via explanations or are you prepared to let others discover issues for themselves? No matter how confident you feel or how well things went last time, it is suggested that you always test each new tool on yourself before you use it with a group.

Suggestions for different contexts

At school

At the start of any project in which you are going to use the problem-solving techniques and tools described here, briefly talk the group through the 4-diamond model. This will help them to see the context and how the diamonds provide a map of the process. During the clarification of the problem statement (diamonds 1 and 2) ensure that the group feel free to change the scope of issue. For example, who is the project owner, are they in the room and are they likely to accept changes? At the idea generation step (diamond 3), choose a tool that is lively. The tool 'metaphor' is a good bet for some fun.

At University

Students are often well versed in their subject matter content but much less aware of creative thinking techniques. Some may be dubious of the value of getting into the 'process' side of group activities as distinct from the 'content' aspects. Research (discovering the unknown) and creativity techniques should be a marriage made in heaven and so all research projects deserve some creative problem solving at the outset such that there is a written problem statement and it has been explored and hopefully modified. If an individual researcher or a team become stuck or feel the need for a fresh perspective during their investigations, then they should know where to find some advice. University students should be encouraged to perform their own facilitation without bringing in middlemen. For example, each student could read up one idea-generation tool, try it out on themselves, and then lead the group through the process.

Commerce/industry

Make sure you understand who is the problem owner. If creativity or product champions exist involve them in some way even if –as is likely – they are not the problem owners. One facilitation tip is to consider letting the organisational 'pain' build up somewhat before facilitation is suggested. In cases where time is often of the essence, the techniques may well be better accepted if it clear that they are being used to lessen the felt pain. At the beginning of a project the participants are more likely to want to make (apparent) progress.

'Blocks' to creativity

Being blocked or at least feeling that you are blocked may have one of the following causes:

- **Emotion** – e.g. that you are too tired or depressed or whatever. Our education may have left us with a strong set of biases about problem solving, e.g. that there is only one right answer; or that everything should be logically related. Some may be fearful of looking foolish or inadequate. Many of us do not like the 'messy' or ambiguous aspects and will try to move through these quickly at the risk of missing a diamond at the bottom of the mud.

- **Personal/cultural perception** – e.g. that the task seems too complex or likely to be required in a specific (cultural) format. The problem solvers immediate environment (i.e. p for 'press') may place unhelpful restrictions or taboos on what can or cannot be achieved.

- **Preferred method of problem solving** – e.g. that you have a strongly favourite set of tools but that in this instance they simply do not seem to be the right tools for the job. It may also be that you define problems quite rigidly, either not knowing or not wanting to use other approaches.

- **Skills/specialisation** – your group may simply lack certain skills or background knowledge.

- **Stress** – is perhaps the commonest cause of blockage. The best response usually is to leave the task for a while and if possible do something that you enjoy doing. Shortage of time is a common source of stress and certainly stress drives out creativity. Many organisations claim they do not have time to apply certain tools but they usually seem to be able to find the time to go back over the problem and solve it better when it crops up again.

- **Lack of imagination** – few people lack imagination if they are sufficiently motivated. It is more common that a group has similar imaginations, for example if they are all electrical engineers or bank managers. The group may therefore need more diversity.

- **Over-confidence**

- **Using inappropriate methods or being poorly led.**

An excellent book about blocks and how to overcome them is *Conceptual Block Busting; a Guide to Better Ideas* by J.L. Adams, published by Penguin. There are also a number of questionnaires available that can be used to identify chronic blocks. These questionnaires (see below) are usually based on the designer's favourite sub-set of the above list of eight types of blocks. The questions are designed to help you identify your most likely or persistent type of block. Thus they may not necessarily be of much use to Joe with his specific block on Tuesday afternoon, but they would help him get in touch with the most typical blocks that his style and preferences would render him prone towards. Three of the most user-friendly of these questionnaires can be obtained as follows:

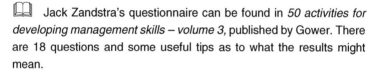 Jack Zandstra's questionnaire can be found in *50 activities for developing management skills – volume 3,* published by Gower. There are 18 questions and some useful tips as to what the results might mean.

📖 Francis and Woodcock's questionnaire, in *People at Work,*

published by University Associates. This consists of 110 questions and uses 11 possible sources of blockage to devise the questions.

📖 Les Jones has developed a 30 question instrument that uses four basic variables. It is called the Jones inventory of barriers to effective problem solving or JIB and also provides a booklet covering the interpretation and feedback. Jones came from the Manchester Business School group that was lead by Tudor Rickards and the inventory can be obtained via MBS or more directly from Les Jones on telephone 020 488 2950.

The material above has dealt mainly with blocks at the individual or group level, although there have been indications that barriers can also exist as a result of organisational/cultural issues. For descriptions of this latter category see chapter 4 about P for 'press'.

Many problem solvers who have been trained in the scientific and technical traditions are biased towards left-brained thinking – i.e. a preference for lots of logic, structure, precision and analysis. It is likely that they entered scientific disciplines and flourished because they already had left-brained skills. Through their lives they are likely to have been further rewarded for these same qualities and skills – thus reinforcing the situation. They may therefore not find it so easy to use some of the right-brained approaches described elsewhere in the book.

The same sort of bias may also apply to people with a right-brained preference who may not like using the highly structured or prescriptive tools, for example, those with lists. The author is reminded that a powerful role model for problem solving – Einstein – seemed very much aware of the need to mix his approaches to creativity. He describes how he used 'mind experiments' to help his imagination. He wouldn't have used terms like 'visualisations' – but his approach seems to contain all the elements of this re-invented technique. So many of the world's greatest inventions trace their break-through moment to the brain working in reverie or a light trance rather than logically engaging the problem in a head-on assault. However, the logical and analytical mode is also required to prepare the mind before the period of break-through and of course afterwards to elaborate the invention. So, it seems to be a matter of being able to switch back and forth between left- and right-brained thinking or speeding up and slowing down the thinking according to Guy Claxton in *Hare Brain – Tortoise Mind.*

Every person who accepts the challenge to facilitate a group through a problem-solving session needs to know how to cope with blocks. They should ideally know about their own most usual blocks and how to cope with them and have some ability to second guess the blocks of others or at least help them to cope.

10

The Inventors Themselves and Some of Their Innovations

The inventors

The Japanese Trade and Industry Ministry recently declared the results of a study they had made into creativity and innovation. They stated that in the 50-year period from 1945, 40% of all key discoveries came from the UK. Of all the commercially viable innovations, 50% came from the UK, 25% from the US and only 5% from Japan. Before the British pat themselves on their creative backs, there is a word of warning. It is undeniable that the British used to be very prolific in having ideas and often patenting them – although this phenomenon seems to be wearing off. As at 1996 (i.e. after the Japanese survey period), the UK ranked only 11th in the world in terms of the numbers of patents filed. It is accepted that using the number of filed patents as a measure of national creativity is far from rigorous, but it is about the best index that has been used.

Unfortunately, the inventor's problems do not end here – after having a great idea, it is still extremely difficult to put that concept into production and/or to realise some profit from your concept. The British Institute of Patentees and Inventors states that of the 4,000 patents taken out each year, only 2% of the ideas reach the market place. The British are known to be notoriously ineffective at following up their ideas and being able to push them into production. Some people argue that it is not the inventors themselves that are at fault but it is mainly the risk-averse character of British moneymen that is a problem. The Japanese study quoted above added that if only the UK had followed up their ideas, they would have added some £156 billion to the gross domestic product of the UK. Some of these great British *ideas* were the PC, the internet, the transistor, the internal combustion engine, Terylene, the video recorder, Viagra, and the jet engine and just think how much of the *innovation* of these concepts has been completed outside the UK.

There are clearly some ethnic cultural forces at work in the fields of creativity and innovation since the Japanese excel in the very area of high quality production where the British have missed so many opportunities. The Japanese creativity however does seem at times to be highly culturally focussed – for example, one of their inventions was a device for alerting the wearer when his trouser fly buttons or zip are undone – but in order to save embarrassment to others rather than to himself. Similarly, the main advantage of the Sony Walkman as stated by the Japanese is that it avoids inconveniencing others; whereas Europeans tend to see the benefits in a more self-centred way.

Trevor Baylis and his clockwork radio

Clearly then, some inventors are motivated partly by a desire to help their fellow beings and Trevor Baylis's work on the clockwork radio falls into this category. Baylis has stated that he watched a TV programme about the AIDS epidemic and was very moved by the suffering and hopelessness. In Africa in particular, there was no cheap way for the people most at risk to receive broadcast information about safer sex. There was little mains electricity in the villages and batteries for a radio were far too expensive. What happened next is an absolutely classical example of the 'eureka' moment of break-through thinking. After watching the TV programme, Baylis fell asleep and dreamt about an old fashioned gramophone – the sort that had a handle and was powered by winding up a spring. He thus had a starting point for his invention and the motivation to sustain him through the long journey ahead. Of all the inventors, Trevor Baylis comes over as the 'nice' one – his compassion for his fellow man seems to provide some of the energy to maintain his progress. He had also previously been involved in the production of household aids for the handicapped. Finally, after immense frustration, rejection and hard development work, a factory opened in South Africa making his clockwork radio. The factory employees a lot of disabled workers which also seems to fit the Baylis ethos. By 1997 there were radio sales of 120,000 per month and various aid agencies now distribute the radio around the world – for example, 47,000 were given to refugees in Kosovo so that they could find out what was going on during the conflict.

Josh Silver and his spectacles

Also in the humane category of invention is the less well known work of Dr. Josh Silver, who has produced very inexpensive spectacles that were first used in any quantity in Ghana. Not only are eye infections common in Africa, but the cost of traditional spectacles can amount to 30% of an individual's annual income. It follows that the poorer Ghanaians simply do not have glasses and when they can't see to work, they do not work and their families suffer. If eye-sight problems strike at an early age, the misery so commonly found in Africa is made even greater. Josh Silver used two silicon lenses for each eye, creating a sealed space between the lenses. This space could be filled and pressurised with water using a hypodermic syringe and then sealed with a small rubber bung. This allowed each lens to be focussed independently by adjusting the water pressure via the syringes. The quality of focus is adjusted by the wearer without the need for a hard-to-find optician and can be re-adjusted whenever necessary to allow for both distant vision and for close up work such as reading or weaving. The first generation of glasses are not so fashionable but have allowed poor sighted farmers to farm and carpenters to return to work so that they can support their families.

However, life in the third world is not always so kind to those bold or desperate enough to try something new. Cheap and widely available energy can help to relieve the grinding poverty in third world countries and, with this target in mind, scientists who tried to introduce hydrogen fuel into the Cameroon thought they might be thanked for their efforts. The electrolysis of water produces hydrogen which needs some careful handling but is a wonderfully clean fuel and more significantly for Africa, can be made simply and in small quantities. However, no-one had anticipated the hostile reaction of those who sold the existing and rival household fuel – butane gas. British managers may complain about the resistance to change, but in this case, the hydrogen man was actually beaten up by the butane boys.

James Dyson and his vacuum cleaners

James Dyson's invention of the 'dual cyclone' or bagless vacuum cleaner in 1979 took over 15 years to develop and this was the first break-through in vacuum-cleaner technology since its inception in 1901. If Trevor Baylis is the 'humane' inventor, Dyson exhibits the dogged determination needed to nurse an innovation through to sales. He is a self styled 'misfit' which obviously means something to him but is less clear to the rest of us – certainly he has had to be very tough in dealing with the predators who wanted to separate him from his invention. His father died when he was 9 years old which, in his case apart from all the personal pain, may or may not have influenced his life as an innovator. This is mentioned only because there are studies which indicate that childhood trauma has been a feature of the lives of many driven and successful people.

Dyson states that he just 'knew' that his dual cyclone machine would be a success eventually and no doubt this inner conviction helped to sustain him through the 'long night' of the innovator. Working from home he made and tested over 5,000 versions of his machine with only his wife's income to keep the family going. Unlike Baylis, Dyson had children to worry about and was very aware of the risks he was taking during the long, gruelling development period. After many setbacks and while fending off dirty tricks by competitors, Dyson eventually took the 'sod you all – I'll produce it myself' route. He wisely held the patent in his own name and had some income from production licenses that he had already granted outside the UK. He could thus easily demonstrate that the dual cyclone worked well and would sell; even so, it was difficult to obtain the funds needed to go into production in the UK. In 1993 he finally began manufacturing the product and within the first year he had sales of £ 2.4 million. This rose to £10 million in the following year and by February 1995, the Dyson machine had become the largest selling cleaner in Britain. Seven years after the product was introduced into Britain, Dyson was selling £191 million worth of machines, taking 33% of the market by volume. His company takes a lot of care of its products and customers and as the author knows from direct experience, they run an extremely effective help line. If the problem cannot be solved over the phone, they will come and fetch your machine and replace it if necessary.

They also care about the environment as well as their own reputation and should your Dyson ever become cranky in its old age they will – at no cost – take it away and re-cycle it. The re-cycled machines are coloured green and re-sold in a cloth bag that can also be used for other purposes. It is clearly a very principled and very excellent organisation. More recently, Dyson has invested in a £20-million research facility, based near Malmesbury. It is staffed by 200 young people – the average age is 25 – some of whom are rumoured to be making prototypes of a very fast spin dryer for domestic use. Given Dyson's disgusting treatment at the hands of competitors and developers, his strong desire to keep his work secret is totally understandable. However it is known that Dyson's R and D facility has already developed an extension of his dual cyclone technology to trap the black sooty deposit that comes from diesel exhaust fumes. His overall success story is a monument to the human capacity to keep going in the face of appalling set backs.

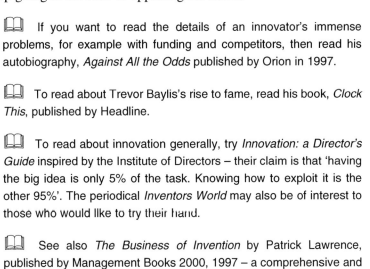

📖 If you want to read the details of an innovator's immense problems, for example with funding and competitors, then read his autobiography, *Against All the Odds* published by Orion in 1997.

📖 To read about Trevor Baylis's rise to fame, read his book, *Clock This*, published by Headline.

📖 To read about innovation generally, try *Innovation: a Director's Guide* inspired by the Institute of Directors – their claim is that 'having the big idea is only 5% of the task. Knowing how to exploit it is the other 95%'. The periodical *Inventors World* may also be of interest to those who would like to try their hand.

📖 See also *The Business of Invention* by Patrick Lawrence, published by Management Books 2000, 1997 – a comprehensive and highly practical manual for inventors.

A key issue for inventors and for problem owners is how best to enhance the two-way flow of ideas and data linking potential solutions to problems. Part of this linking process has been called 'opportunity spotting' and the book with this title by McLennon (published by Gower) may also be of interest. Many people now know that market-led problem solving is financially more successful than technology-led approaches which start with potential solutions and then try to find or create markets for the ideas.

However, you cannot stop people having ideas, whether they come from a laboratory that produces a surprising result or from finding a plant or bug in some remote corner that seems to have novel effects.

There is for example a gene in certain jellyfish that enables the host to glow – can anyone think of an application for this? The gene can also be transplanted into other living organisms which will often also be able to self-illuminate. Another process that is creating new markets is called 'convergence', which is the cross fertilisation of two or more apparently separate streams of technology or even administration. For example, television and computers are currently converging to deliver entertainment via video systems on the internet or data handling capacity via cable TV monitors.

Perhaps we need a new breed of opportunity spotter or arbitrageur (a form of benign venture capitalist) who will fit together problems and appropriate solutions – albeit at a price. The trick at the national level is to find a way of ensuring that the price is reasonable and/or that money could be made available for ideas that deserve funding. Other ways of achieving this synthesis would be to build on the concept of the invention machine (chapter 7), for example by expanding the databases into non-technical areas and adding some techniques from the expanding area of knowledge management. Unfortunately the invention machine databases still only lead you towards a workable solution; it still needs human intelligence to make the final connection.

Another approach for facilitating inventions would be to build on Trevor Baylis's concept of an Innovation Academy, or at least to do more to enhance networks of people – preferably synergistic meetings of some people with problems, some with solutions, some with finance and some facilitators who understand the processes of creativity and innovation. Baylis and Dyson recently joined forces to approach the Department of Trade and Industry to press their ideas for more stimulation for innovation. One step in a good direction has been taken by The Sunday Times who operate the Enterprise Network in association with the DTI. The Network's activities can be viewed on **www.enterprisenetwork.co.uk** or telephoned on 01869 337 004. Another worthy organisation that funds creativity and helps innovation is NESTA – the National Endowment for Science, Technology and the Arts. David Putnam is a leading light and in May 2000, after receiving £200 million in Lottery funding, NESTA gave £2.8 million in 28 separate awards spread throughout its three main categories.

Part of the issue of stimulating innovation is the need to further protect the inventors. 'First Tuesday' is a network club that finds investors for inventors. They have, however, had to strengthen security after complaints of thought theft.

American patent law has covered business methods as well as products for several years. The UK's Patent Office is soliciting views from the business community as to whether they would like to see UK/European law similarly extended.

Two recent services are already helping inventors to protect their intellectual property. First Use (**www.firstuse.com**) says it can digitally finger-print, time stamp and register any file to strengthen legal documentation. First Use was launched in 2000 and claims clients in fifty professions, spread over sixty countries. The Evergreen Copyright Index offers inventors a range of services. For example, for £50 per item, ECI can supply evidence that the concept was registered on a particular date. Application forms can be downloaded from **www.copyrightprotection.net**.

This 'issue' (i.e. it is both a problem and a large opportunity) of stimulating innovation can be resolved by the methods described elsewhere in the book and readers are invited to tackle it themselves. It is suggested that you first clarify your own perspective on the issue by writing down a problem statement or statements. You should then do some investigation (maybe read the books by Baylis and Dyson, together with Lawrence's manual) because 'luck favours the prepared mind'. Then select one of the idea generation tools and see what pops out. The discerning reader will not expect instant results and may be happy to return to the theme when either on a long or boring journey, in an uninteresting meeting, in the bath, jogging or even while asleep.

As long as you believe that it might work, all you have to do is to repeat the problem statement to yourself a few times before falling asleep. Thereafter one of the tricky bits is to be able to edit your dreams on waking up. It is hopeless if you have to get up immediately and perform some other set of activities – try to arrange to wake early and remain in your sleeping position while you run through the salient parts of the dream. It helps some people to make some notes.

Another tricky bit about the interpretation of the dream is that it is often simply acting as a stimulus to jolt your thinking. The parts of the brain involved while sleeping usually produce a very symbolic output and you may be left with the further problem of unscrambling your own symbolism. The apparent message of the dream may have to be treated as if it was a metaphor for a solution – it may therefore have to be modified to convert it into a workable solution. Assume for a moment that you dreamed of a beautiful and sensuous member of the opposite sex called Desire – one way to proceed is to answer the question 'what has Desire got to do with stimulating innovation?' You may need to repeat this question for any other key features of the dream; you will also probably need to play with your thoughts – mould them, sculpt them, spin them, hammer them or blow them up until they form something that you can build on.

Alternatively, like Trevor Baylis in the case above, you may dream of a more direct solution to your problem. Invention is strewn with legends, most of which cannot be proven, but they usually illustrate an important aspect of creativity or innovation. Accordingly, it is said that around the turn of the 19th century, an American was working hard to develop the first automatic sewing machine. The particular micro-problem was how to create a stitch – that is to manipulate the sewing thread to apparently pass around curved surfaces and to engage back on itself in the form of a knot that would simply not unravel under tension. The American dreamt of being hunted by foreigners with spears. However – and this is why you need to pay serious attention to your dreams – he later realised that the spears had odd little holes in the metal tip – just like a modern needle. 'Eureka!'

the break-through was made – all it needed was some development work to perfect the interaction of the needle and a reciprocating shuttle both carrying threads at right angles to each other and the modern sewing machine was born. It is easy to dismiss this dream-stuff as silly and indeed it may not work at all easily and not at all for some people, but so many inventors have had great ideas whilst either in a light trance or asleep that it is worth considering.

In preparing this book, one of the author's dilemmas within the authoring system was how to file creative ideas – essentially should they be filed mainly under their technology of origin or filed under the market they might serve? Since one does not know what all the potential markets might be and the very essence of creativity is novelty, some of the data has to be retained under their technology. However, to stimulate market-oriented thinking and innovation the more workable connections need also to be listed in market groupings where the payoff is more probable. Accordingly, in a home PC with a relatively small memory, examples of laser applications need to be filed under 'lasers in medicine' and 'lasers in telecommunications' as well as 'lasers for cutting'.

Accordingly, the next section presents a selection of recent inventions in medicine that hopefully are interesting in their own right and refer to the human condition but also illustrate some of the principles involved in innovation The author discarded examples of 'chemicals' leading to medical innovations because this goes back to the very origins of medicine as a coherent profession and accordingly had an 'ancient' feel to it. Instead the following routes to innovation in medicine have been chosen:

- applications of material science
- applications of radiation
- an example of robotics
- an analysis of a trend in medical innovation.

Some applications of material science in medicine

This section was also of personal interest to the author since, as a young chemist, he had worked with several of the relevant materials and in several cases 'it could have been me' who made the break-through. It has also been interesting to see what has changed over the last thirty years.

Case No 1 – going to the dentist

In 1960, a dentist friend of the author outlined the specifications for 'a substance, possibly a plastic, to fill teeth'.

Further specifications were that it had to be non-toxic and stable to the micro-organisms, acidity and warmth of the mouth. It also had to be reproducible in a range of tooth colours.

Not surprisingly, cost was not mentioned since the use of the then common mercury amalgams were already concerning some of the more discerning dentists. Some sort of polymerisation reaction seemed to fit the bill. Stable starting material could be squirted into the tooth cavity and somehow converted quickly into a strong plastic. Unfortunately most polymerisation reactions in those days required relatively high temperatures or pressures and some reactive catalyst – all of which were out of the question. Polymerisation by radiation seemed to be a possible route – but unfortunately the problem was left there. In 1999, it was heartening to read that a group at Bristol University were announcing a filling that could last forever. Like many break-throughs, it had two components. In this case the University also had a separate unit that had achieved improvements with light emitting diodes and these provided the critical technology. They were able to produce a very high intensity of light by focussing it through a cone, which was small enough to be operated inside a patient's mouth. The other key component was in the choice of a polymer that is able to bind onto and into the porous structure of a tooth to form a very strong bond. Previous plastics had merely filled the tooth's cavity – rather like using polyester filler to mend a hole in a car body or window frame. The magic chemical monomer and silica filler is injected directly into the cavity and 30 seconds exposure to the light emitting diode creates the strong and durable bonds.

Case No 2 – mending bones

As a chemist in the 1960s, the author had also worked with the then relatively new carbon fibres. They were immensely strong – hence the focus of interest in them – and it was known that the main factor limiting their application was not the qualities of the fibres themselves, but the understanding by designers and engineers of how their characteristics could be exploited.

Often in combination with other materials, they have since been applied very successfully in bridges, racing cars, aircraft wings, skis, and other relatively high value products. As their use increases, a virtuous cycle commences in which the greater volume demanded for new applications lowers the manufacturing costs and the cheaper the product becomes, which in turn attracts more users and so on. The author was pleased to see that in 1994 – after ten years of development – a human hip designer was utilising both the chemical stability and hence long life, as well as the physical flexibility of carbon fibres. The conventional approach used mainly metal hip replacements that were glued to the existing leg bone. Dr John Bradley – the carbon fibre innovator – knew that the new metal hip sometimes broke the surrounding bone because the metal lacked the flexibility needed in the body's dynamic system of tissues and fluids. The carbon fibre composite however distributes the stresses in the human body in a similar way to the dispersal of stresses in composite structures in vibrating aircraft wings or snow skis chattering over icy slopes. As with so many innovations, Dr Bradley has encountered resistance from surgical units who do not want to try something new. Like the example in Case No 1, he is also having to cope with the problem of the initial cost barrier.

Case No 3 – growing bones to order

Back in the 1960s, the author had worked with various polyester polymers – trying to make imitation leather and self-washing clothes. The ideal customer for the latter was seen to be the travelling sales-person who only had a limited change of clothes and yet was away from home for several weeks. The concept was to attach a suitable enzyme to a polymer and produce garments in the usual way. The clothes would then simply be thrown into a basin of water at the end of a day's wear and the dirt-consuming enzyme would chomp away at the sweat stains. Like many great ideas, it almost worked – one major obstacle was that the collars and cuffs of shirts needed such a high concentration of enzyme that they produced rashes on the sensitive parts of the skin of the trial wearers. Around the same time, the author was also designing and producing biodegradable polymers, which led 30 years later to pleasure at hearing about the next innovation.

In 1999, a group of bio-engineers at the Mayo clinic in Minnesota have dramatically upgraded various features of a polyester in attempts to control bone growth. The conventional approach to rebuilding broken bones usually involved several separate operations as surgeons gradually homed in on the correct dimensions of the bone replacement and regularly checked bone fusion. The bone graft also often came from another part of the same patient's body in order to avoid the body's rejection of tissue from another donor.

This multi-operation approach increases the total amount of patient discomfort and is an expensive way to use scarce hospital resources. The new paradigm involves implanting a shaped plastic pattern and inducing bone cells to grow into this specified shape inside the body. A good metaphor for modern tissue replacement is that it is akin to building a house. One needs permanent building bricks and temporary scaffolding for both processes. The two key parts of the Mayo clinic work have been firstly, the identification of a suitable biodegradable plastic, which forms the pattern to guide the new bone growth and support the tissue during this process. This plastic was carefully designed slowly to biodegrade in the body. The polymer chemists thus had to achieve a delicate balance between maintaining sufficient of the falling strength of the supporting mould and the opposing need for it to degrade and flush away from the site. The second feature was to incorporate human growth hormone into the plastic mould – this hormone communicates with nearby healthy bone cells, which then diffuse into the pattern. The new bone gradually replaces the plastic and eventually fills the exact shape of the original fracture void; it also knits well onto existing bone and tissue. This is an example of a growing trend in medicine to grow human organs to fit accident sites precisely rather than to try to repair or graft external tissue.

Many readers will have seen the photograph of the bio-engineered mouse with a human ear growing on its back. A more sophisticated application is to use human stem cells – this is the name given to the cells very early in their growth cycle. They can be used as the basic building blocks to be converted into other types of cells. The stem cells have not yet been 'told' what type of a cell they are to become and can still be induced to develop into say bone or hair or eye cells. At the Harvard medical school, tissue engineers used these techniques to grow a version of a human bladder in 1999. Their second project was to produce a prototype of a womb and their third target was the production of the more complex human kidney. Another group at the University of Toronto is trying to produce whole limbs to exactly fit accident patients. They also plan to grow working versions of breasts, hearts, and even a liver.

Innovations involving robots in medicine

This example discusses some developments achieved since 1998 at the University of Tokyo. It is not surprising that the push to develop markets for robots comes from Japan since they already have so much expertise in that area. Correspondingly, part of the pull comes from Japanese culture in which it is the children's duty to look after their elderly relatives. However, with many more women now in employment, this has become increasingly difficult.

Another attractive feature of the development for Japanese society is that the robots can improve the quality of life for the elderly patients; for example by turning the pages of a book or newspaper or fetching a photograph of a loved one. The system is designed for the elderly and sick and so an array of sensors and robots has been clustered around a typical hospital bed. On the medical side, many detecting instruments are involved in monitoring the vital life signs and highlighting dangers to a central control unit. These life sign sensors are similar to those in the list involved in the section below that have also been incorporated into intelligent clothing. Additionally for bed bound patients, there is the important facility to monitor bedsores. The mattress incorporates more then 200 sensors and a computer analyses the length of time that a patient remains in any one position. A pre-set level control triggers an alarm when a patient needs to be turned.

Trying to encourage all their patients to venture out of the bed, the room has also been made as safe as possible. For example, pressure sensors on floor tiles can monitor patient movement and signal an alarm if a fall is detected. On the quality of life aspects of the design, patients merely have to point at an object such as a TV in order to operate it. Curtains, lighting, and room or bed temperature are controlled by the patient in a similar way. Slave robots will fetch favourite items such as books, food and audio or videotapes.

The UK's first robot-assisted operation took place on 6 December 2000. It was performed by Professor Darzi on Mikhail Hanna's gallstone at St Mary's Hospital, Paddington. The robotic slave wields scalpels and other surgeon's tools that are controlled via joy-sticks. Hand tremors are filtered out by a PC. Mr Hanna is alive and well and required fewer stitches than a conventional cut would require.

Some trends in medicine

A trend is akin to the current paradigm and illustrates the way in which the dominant groups are thinking and performing at the moment. The marketing of a wide range of home testing kits is one of the current trends in medicine. The original selling proposition filled the need to test in secret and this ensured that pregnancy tests were a commercial success. There followed some other home kits that relied on simple, proven and robust technology such as cholesterol testing, fending off heart problems, and using nicotine substitutes to wean smokers off cigarettes.

However, it is now known that other groups in society do not readily go and visit their GP even when they are not feeling fully fit – for example, men have relatively much lower attendance records.

Another factor driving innovation in home kits is the dislike or even fear of having invasive tests such as being injected by needle or having a body sample removed by surgery. In many cases it is not so much a matter of a fear that can be defined, but more of a nagging doubt in the back of the mind, but this can be enough to delay a visit to the needle-wielding medical practitioner. Children also are a difficult group to inject and accordingly testing kits that rely on saliva samples and devices that deliver medicines under the skin without using needles have become much more popular.

Not surprisingly the medical practitioners also do not enjoy a life of creating fear in their patients and have also pushed for the development of novel delivery and test methods. Workers at the

University of Mississippi spotted a marketplace opportunity and have developed a saliva test for breast cancer. Human salivary glands produce nearly one litre of saliva per day and it is safer to handle than blood. Saliva tests have now been developed for measles, HIV and various drugs including alcohol levels. Tests for detecting hepatitis A and B are also under development. The Mayo clinic in Minnesota who already had an impressive record of innovation, turned their attention in 1997 to the plight of diabetes sufferers. One of the problems for diabetics is that they need to measure their blood sugar levels up to five times a day and this has traditionally been achieved via a blood sample taken by needle. The break-through achieved at the Mayo clinic was the discovery that just below the skin is a clear fluid that carries small amounts of blood sugar but its ratio to other body fluids is similar to that found in the blood. Accordingly and importantly, these samples yield the same data as the blood samples. Sufficient amounts of this fluid can be obtained by using a very small needle that only just penetrates the skin.

Another recent trend is the approach towards the less or even non-invasive procedures for delivering medicines into the body. In the 1980s, it was known that although the skin is water proof, chemicals such as dimethyl sulphoxide were very rapidly absorbed through the skin and could carry medically active agents with them. Painless doses of vaccines were administered to children using this technique before fears arose about the longer term side effects of the sulphoxide carrier. In the 1990s, duPont marketed a 'gun' that can be used for the self administration of medicines. This gun achieves the painless penetration of the skin by using a compressed water jet into whose stream the drug can be added. The Victoria College of Pharmacy in Melbourne is investigating the fundamentals of 'spray-on medicine'. They have developed a three-inch plastic applicator (called a 'puffer') that will deliver medicines easily below the skin within one minute. They have also developed a four-part mixture to their spray that consists of a propellant (as found in common aerosol cans); a solvent to dissolve the drug; the drug itself and lastly a penetration enhancer. The penetration enhancers work like the sulphoxide in the previous example to pull the drug through the skin, but Victoria College claim to have developed their own variants that do not have unwanted side-effects.

165

They have already tested the delivery of male contraceptives and HRT drugs and have found that their system has advantages for some users. A competing delivery system involves the use of sticky patches that contain the active medical ingredients – for example, agents involved in helping the wearers give up smoking or those needing a regular but low dose of drugs for a heart condition. However, some patch wearers develop a reaction against the patch which can lead to skin blisters, whereas so far the puffer system has not caused skin reactions.

Creativity and innovation in the Armed forces

Some readers may not applaud military innovation. However, it does illustrate some aspects of the motivation to invent and, more practically via spin-offs into civilian areas, it shows how ideas spread through society and are improved by modification. This is especially true for the huge US military budgets, but even in the UK, there are methods being developed to recharge batteries located in our shoes as we walk. The military applications arena also shows how separate innovations incorporate each other and hybridise in a form of chain reaction, producing very large numbers of possible new products. For example, the military scientists have imported civilian encryption techniques to safeguard their communications. They have also reversed some of these concepts to allow the easier identification of friendly and enemy troops. The Armed forces have always had stealth technology on their agendas since the ancient Britons first used woad. Initially applied to aircraft, it is now used for ships, tanks, and even individual soldiers. One alternative to hiding your troops is to employ virtual imaging technology to create the illusion of other hostile forces.

The greatest single factor driving most of these applications is the use of information technology and the miniaturisation of the associated hardware. Examples below also show how some of the tools of genetic engineering have been press-ganged into military service along with the use of robots. The US military have also been aided by early access to spin-off techniques developed in turn from NASA funding. Lightweight foods developed for astronauts are now supplied to combat troops who can also receive special supplements before going into battle.

Apart from the very significant increase in resources available to the military, their processes of creativity and innovation are no different from those used in other fields. It is also possible that the 'backs against the wall' feeling created during periods of conflict may heighten the motivation of the creators and lessen the resistance and over-critical evaluation of some of the decision makers.

Well known examples of creativity from the Second World War are the Barnes-Wallis 'bouncing bomb' used against the Eider and Moehne dams in the Ruhr; the development of radar and the code-breaking efforts of the teams at Bletchley. More recently, break-throughs have come – as in other fields – from the application of new materials (e.g. the plastic tank) and robotics. Defence spending funds the military innovations but the upside is the chance to spin-off applications and materials into the civilian sphere. For example, from the battlefield robot surgeon comes the opportunity to apply this technology to remote areas such as the Australian outback and the Canadian tundra. In the USA, military surgeons and robotics experts have developed software and hardware that can perform operations on the battlefield. The remote surgeon can even see the patient and the robot deploys arms that can be made to mimic the surgeon's movements via sophisticated telemetry.

The 'intelligent' medical patches incorporated into military uniforms (used to relay data about wounds, to apply antibiotics and provide nourishment) have also led directly to the following civilian applications. Patches can also provide key materials for athletes, for example those in long distance events – marathon runners, bi/tri-athlon participants, swimmers, and mountaineers etc.

The intelligent stretcher first developed for the battlefield is now being introduced for search and rescue operations – for example those following disasters such as earthquakes. One version of the stretcher known as 'elstat' is able to help ventilate and intubate patients and is even able to access their medical records. In case there is only a single operator available, some of the functions such as the heart defibrillator can be voice operated and remote experts can be accessed for world class medical advice. In the USA, these stretchers are now available for the equivalent of about £80.

Smart battlefield uniforms have also been developed by the US Army soldier centre at Natick, Massachusetts. These incorporate arm and leg tourniquets that can apply air pressure to limit loss of blood. The skin-tight suits also contain a network of fine wires that allow a remote sensor to identify both where the soldier is located (using global positioning) and also where in the body they have been injured.

The outer textile surface can also be made to act like a video screen so that the soldiers could merge automatically with their changing surroundings. The colours do not come from surface pigments as with traditional camouflage but are produced electronically via fibre optics and thus can mimic a wide range of backgrounds. Other stealth technology, in one case using a modified coal dust, is used to minimise the heat signature emitted by the soldier.

Under-clothing can incorporate not only heating but also hollow fibres that can deliver clotting factors and other medicines. Yet other fibres built into the clothing can be made to support the muscles adding to leg strength.

A miniature spectrometer of the type initially developed for space exploration will be able to detect the presence of blood in the uniform. This is complimented by pinhead sized microphones that are able to detect the audio difference between an aerated chest wound that creates a 'sucking' noise and say a broken bone. All this injury data can be analysed both by battlefield medics close by and at a remote control centre – both able to confer if necessary about triage decisions.

Improvements to blood-clotting applications are already being used to help civilian road traffic accident patients. Much of creative invention comes from acute observation and it was this opportunity spotting by battlefield medics in the Falklands that has led to the following advances in casualty care. The medics noticed that wounded soldiers left overnight on the battlefield had higher recovery rates than, for example, those known for the hostilities in Vietnam. The effect was finally tracked down to the beneficial overnight cooling that helps to preserve both the brain and body tissue. At around two to three degrees centigrade, the body's messages that normally instruct cells to self-destruct are inhibited. The Russians had previously tried to slow down mortality by experimenting with dogs that had been cooled. Unfortunately they cooled the dogs too much and the experiments failed – however by luck, the overnight temperatures in the Falklands were in the right range to allow the effect to operate. A similar form of suspended animation had been reported from Haiti and was caused by powerful fish venom that was used in certain voodoo rites. Military medics thought that it could be used in hotter climates for casualties but unfortunately the dose required for successful hibernation is far too close to the lethal dose for practical application. However, the general concept already has a civilian road traffic application. These traffic patients are given a 200ml chest injection of cold blood that buys precious time to enable them to be transported more safely to hospital.

Much of the 'power' and enhanced functionality of battlefield clothing has come from wearable computers. The batteries to run these applications are likely to be recharged via piezo-electric devices stored in the heels of the wearers' boots. Our old friend Trevor Baylis (inventor of the clockwork radio) was involved in initial studies and the UK government's military applications and evaluation unit – DERA – have developed the concept of battery-charging footwear. Future soldiers will use this to power their own two-way communications with colleagues and with their command centre as well as head-up displays on their visors. These visors will show not only the topography of what Wellington called 'the other side of the hill' – i.e. the hidden ground ahead – but also the disposition of mines. They will also be able to download modifications to their plan of attack – all powered from their boots.

Soldiers will also receive more hardware; for example the gun that fires around corners is already on order in the USA. It is called the OICW gun (Objective Individual Combat Weapon) and it should enable the infantry to have a higher fire power and yet be less reliant on artillery. The OICW will have automatic range finding and bullets can be set to explode not on impact but at pre-set distances – hence its capacity to deliver around corners.

The American military has invested massive funds to bring their forces into the digital age. Many readers will have seen video footage of smart bombs used against the Iraqis and in the Balkans. Some of the motivation for these came from the lessons learned in the 1940s from which it was estimated that the average bomb fell a quarter of a mile from its target. Consequently, in order to be sure of hitting a target measuring 10 foot square – 30,000 bombs had to be deployed.

Air power is moving further into space, as this is the current high ground that provides military superiority. However, many military developments are related to aqua-warfare – very silent, very deep and fast submarines have been developed. These use materials such as concrete to withstand the water pressures. They may also use the torpedo that fires vertically and achieves very high speed by wrapping its surfaces with air to reduce hydrodynamic drag.

The previous use of animals in military applications is now yielding to the applications of robotics – which can also save human lives. For example, in the 1940s, Russians trained dogs to crawl under German vehicles, with explosives strapped to their backs (naturally they used Pavlovian techniques to train the dogs). Similarly, just after the Second World War, the Americans used dolphins both to deliver and detect mines. More recently however a miniature surveillance 'eye' inspired by insect studies has been incorporated into a flying drone for battlefields.

The miniaturisation involved also makes this a good approach to examining collapsed buildings for trapped humans, for example, after earthquakes. Another example of miniaturisation is the electronic chip that can now be used to steer an animal which can also be equipped with minute audio or video components that can be used to spy on the enemy. Japanese scientists have already achieved significant progress with this approach by controlling cockroaches with electronic packages glued to their backs. Scientists at Reading University are meanwhile trying to improve these types of control processes by directly linking the electronics to the creature's brain.

Bionics is the field of creativity that does not use animals and plants directly, but creates products and processes by imitating certain aspects of their functionality. Also at Reading University, scientists have applied some of the principles of bionics after they discovered to their surprise that some birds' feathers could be used to absorb the power of the impact from a bullet. The intricate structure of the feather developed by evolution over hundreds of thousands of years would be far too expensive to manufacture in a man-made process.

However, it could be used to replace Kevlar (a Nylon derivative) for bullet proof vests for police or soldiers.

In the USA, the Draper laboratories in Massachusetts applied some bionics after noticing that the tuna was a most efficient swimmer. They have developed an 8-foot, first generation robotic fish that mimics the tuna's swimming movements. The idea is to use it in military applications in place of midget submarines utilising the robot's small size and great speed.

The anti-mine movement has spawned some effective ideas as follows. The mine detectors need non-conventional energy sources, either to ensure they do not run out of energy in the middle of a search or to avoid triggering mines that have mine survival devices which detect external energy sources. In one recent innovation, the swinging motion of the detector itself can be used to provide the power needed to operate it.

Plastics can now be sprayed onto mines to render them less dangerous and, borrowing ideas from the field of bacteriology, this allows some explosives to be identified and subsequently defused by bacteria. To detect mines, bacteria have been developed that glow when they are brought in contact with explosives such as TNT. One civilian application for this approach is its use at sea and air ports to detect terrorist activities involving explosives and it is also possible that bacteria could be used to detect certain classes of drugs. The subsequent step of destroying explosives by bacteria has been developed at the University of Cardiff.

The Achilles heel of TNT and related explosives is that they contain the chemical function known as the nitro group. Certain nitrogen loving bacteria have now been isolated that munch their way through this active part of the explosive. The Cardiff group thinks that, via genetic modification, it would be possible to produce other bacteria that would be able to destroy a wider range of explosives.

Novel ideas for fabrics and clothes

As a young chemist, the author was involved in a project which could have revolutionised the traditional clothing industry by applying what were then new ideas from polymer science. The traditional methods of making clothes were both energy and manpower intensive and the latter was becoming a serious problem in the UK's capacity to compete with cheaper imports. The conventional approach involved converting a chemical monomer into polymer, spinning this through a small die to make yarn, weaving this into cloth and finally tailoring this into clothes. The big new idea was to spray a tailor's dummy with a monomer which was light sensitive, and irradiate this to produce a cross-linked polymer which would yield 'off the dummy' clothes.

Conventional fabric has a 3-dimensional structure, which gives it some of its desirable properties such as the 'drape' of silk or the warmth of acrylic. The 3-D structure of our new process would be produced by incorporating some filler such as frozen crystals that would give the new wonder polymer a texture after the crystals had been melted.

Unfortunately the product never made it to the market, but meanwhile the UK had lost a lot of its clothing industry to the Far Eastern competition. However, it is delightful to see (as described below) that in the new millennium there are still plenty of ideas for sprucing up the clothing and fabric markets.

Intelligent clothes

The examples below illustrate the 'combinative' route to innovation in which a traditional market becomes diffused with add-on materials and processes from another younger sector – in this case, often from information technology.

- The smart bra senses the sudden pulse rate rise when its wearer fears an attack and triggers an alarm. The device can distinguish between a heart suddenly beating faster due to panic or a medical condition and the steadier increase involved in innocent excitements such as exercise. Nokia is interested in adding the capacity for the bra to dial for assistance and for its position to be identified by global positioning. It is estimated that the ensemble will cost about £30.

- In the USA, sensor fibres have been woven into fabric to monitor the medical condition of both the elderly and the very young and a market is thought to exist for protecting premature babies. In Finland, you can buy an intelligent survival suit. For about 10 years, skiers have been able to have a survival alarm fitted within the heel of their boot. However, the Finnish jacket will contain 16 Mb of memory stitched into the fabric to monitor heart rate, body temperature and other functions. When a dangerous situation has been diagnosed, the jacket automatically emits a warning signal. Unless this is cancelled by the wearer, the jacket calls for help and identifies its location using global positioning technology. It will cost about £270 and can be ordered via **www.reima.fi.**

● An electrically conductive fibre mesh woven into a fibre is capable of sensing pressure placed on the fabric and the following products are envisaged. Wearers with low speech ability – especially children – could communicate by tapping the material, which can be linked to a voice synthesiser or VDU. It is predicted that clothes will start to exhibit a wide range of electronically enabled devices and garments containing the mesh could easily incorporate a telephone keypad. It would also be quite simple to have a football shirt that informed the referees when it had been tugged by more than a certain amount. The basic mesh material in all of these products can be washed or handled quite roughly without damage and can be mass-produced cheaply. What other functions or benefits would you be prepared to pay for? The fabric could be taken up by the leisure industry for talking books, or for chairs containing a remote TV control. In the security market – carpets could detect intruders.

● The smart kitchen apron could also soon be available. The key component is the embedded microphone, which can be voice activated to control kitchen gadgets. It could also be used to call the family to the table or to eavesdrop on guests in the dining room to see if they are ready for the next course.

● In the health sector, British doctors have already produced 'cuffs' that can predict arterial disease by monitoring blood flow. In 1995, the British company Creative Expressions developed a shirt that would give warnings about exposure to sun burn by incorporating chemicals that change colour on exposure to various amounts of ultra violet rays. Let us hope that they had an export market in mind! It is relatively easy for 'smart' clothing to monitor a wide range of body functions that can give early warnings as pre-set danger levels are approached.

The technology is not the issue, the problem is to develop the market – will people be prepared to pay for the convenience and can sufficient added value, such as security, be demonstrated? The functions that can already be monitored include – heart rhythms, circulation data, blood-oxygen levels, glucose levels for diabetes, alcohol and cholesterol levels. It is also already possible to warn epileptics of imminent seizures.

The miniaturisation of these sensors progresses each year such that in the USA, bio-engineers have developed a medical shirt that monitors 10 body functions. A smaller version even fits onto a shirt-tail. The medical data can be transmitted continuously via telephone links to a central PC. Alternatively, on your next visit to the doctor you simply take the shirt to be read by scanners.

It would also be possible to go beyond simple monitoring of a given condition and arrange to take some remedial action via the garment itself. For monitoring a single medical condition, it is already possible to buy sensors from US suppliers – for example, the Instromedix Corporation sell the Heartwatch that monitors your heart and sends an emergency signal if pre-set limits have been exceeded.

Smart pants have been developed by the MIT Media laboratory that sense the indoor temperature and can signal the central heating boiler to adjust its output.

- The fashion industry is interested in the bikini which incorporates an MP3 audio player, a shirt containing a mobile phone and the ski jacket that warms up its wearer and can warn when other skiers approach too close. A proximity sensor could also light the rear of the jacket to warn off the closing skier – what message would you like to send? It is expected that the batteries used to power these devices will soon be powered by the body's own heat.

- Nicholas Negroponte founded the Media lab at the Massachusetts Institute of Technology (MIT) in Boston in 1986. The Media lab must be the world's greatest source of new ideas and it was Negroponte himself who, in the 1960s, first talked about electronic books that could be charged up with a given text that could be erased and replaced an infinite number of times – all without wasting paper. So what is it about MIT that is so innovative ? It is a centre of excellence of world class that is in a virtuous cycle of being able to attract both big funding and the most intelligent undergraduates, graduates and staff. Gordon Brown was so impressed during a recent visit that he wanted to grow a version in the UK. He initially tried to persuade MIT to establish an off-shoot in the UK. The founding fathers refused this but agreed to a joint venture with Cambridge University which will attract Government funding of £70 million. MIT boasts 46 Nobel laureates and its past students have created immense wealth and employment in the ventures they have created. An estimate of this wealth creation would place MIT as the 24th world body in GDP terms, on a par with Thailand. Teaching and learning are taken very seriously and all science undergraduates must also take a non-technical subject as part of the degree curriculum.

- Negroponte has also stated that the shoe is the most under-exploited part of every-day clothing. Trevor Baylis already knows how to recharge batteries from a piezo-electric device contained within the heel. As you walk, the flexing of the shoe by the foot energises the piezo materials, which produce electricity as they bend. Negroponte not only wants to put computing power into the heel; he also predicts the use of the body itself as a network. He can see the widespread use of 'body area networks' to match the current 'local area networks' already common in offices for linking PCs together to share computing power. The media lab has shown that the body conducts data 'pretty well – up to 100,000 bits per second'.

- Novel fabrics are not only entering the clothing markets; architects and engineers are using them to produce permanent tent-like structures that can be as strong as traditional buildings but visually more exciting. They can also be more easily coated with polymers such as PTFE (non-stick teflon) to make them almost self-cleaning or at least significantly easier and cheaper to clean than stone or brick structures. The surface coatings can also lead to soundproofing and could be made to change colour. Inside the home, curtains can be made to convert household noise into music to suit your particular mood.

Produce your own innovation

Iris Whyte is 65 and is overjoyed that her Snappy Sox invention is now being sold in over 30 Marks and Spencers shops. As is so often the case, the original concept developed from an annoyance that festered into creativity. Iris became increasingly frustrated that her daughter lost so many single socks at boarding school so she invented a simple way of snapping them together. As you might expect, she struggled for years to find a developer (see the diagram of the 'long, dark night of the innovator' in chapter 3). Like James Dyson (as at October 2000 Dyson was taking the Hoover organisation to the cleaners for infringing his patents), Iris also had the good sense to patent her idea.

Patents
Patents were first developed in the 15th century by Venetian glass workers and the concept spread through Europe as these workers changed their work place. The earliest English patent was awarded in 1449 by Henry VI to John Utyman who was himself a Flemish glass maker. This granted him a 20 year monopoly to squeeze the value from the idea.

Registering a patent can take up to 18 months. Firstly your idea is checked to see whether it is original. To be patentable, the concept must be original as well as an advance on existing technology. The inventor must also be able to show that the product can be manufactured. Then the inventor or his or her agent contacts the Home Office to ensure that the new idea does not contravene an existing patent. If the great idea is still viable, the Patent Office will issue a patent after you have paid the hefty fees. It can easily cost over £5,000 to test your idea and obtain patent protection. To develop the product into a production-friendly mode can easily require ten times that figure and this is why so many inventors are either hugely in debt or seek out Venture Capitalists to take over their project. To establish a production line can cost up to another £100,000 and this is before the hunt for market channels and distribution networks. It is not surprising that ideas take an average of seven years to come to market. Note that books and songs are covered by the simpler procedure known as copyright. Readers will remember that during the early creative phase of producing ideas, the 'J' word – judgement – is banned. However, during product development, it is an excess of evaluation that is required. Below are a few humourous examples of products that could have done with a bit more critical thinking before they were launched.

● It was a wonderful idea to give American school children a free pencil with the motto 'Too cool to use drugs' engraved on the side. However, after the pencil sharpener had been used a bit, parents and teachers were horrified to see the abbreviated message 'cool to use drugs'. Perhaps they should have spent a bit more and given the children an emblazoned biro.

● Other more expensive mistakes include:
  • Unilever produced a Persil power powder that shredded underpants.
  • The new Formula Shell petrol corroded some types of car engines.
  • A new Pepsi flopped.
  • In 1992, Hoover offered free air travel as a promotional campaign to sell its vacuum cleaners. However, this became an offer that nearly destroyed the company – they made £30 million in extra sales, but paid out £48 million in air tickets.
  • The A-class Baby Benz produced by Mercedes was a flop.

● Pete Goss and the Team Philips super catamaran were able to draw inspiration from the view that ground-breaking innovations such as their boat should expect a few set backs. You may remember that in a shaking-down cruise off the Scillies, one bow broke and then their mast had seating problems in an Atlantic trial. Eventually, in late 2000, the whole boat was lost in an Atlantic gale it could not contend with.

177

- Some 'mistakes' can be quite beneficial if you are very observant – for example, the pharmaceuticals company Merck produced a drug with what seemed to be the very unwelcome side effect of producing large amounts of hair growth – yes, they converted it into a cure for baldness.

- One feels sorry for scientists whose mother tongue is not English, since most science is conducted in this language. For example, the Japanese researcher could be forgiven for confusing the chemical symbol for yttrium (Y). However, as a result of his 'mistake', he produced the world's most magnetic substance.

Have a go yourself

If 11-year olds can do it, why can't you? André Samuel and Costas Pitas from Latymer School in London have developed a sensor that triggers an alarm when a plant needs feeding. The system switches on a light until the plant has been watered. A warning is sounded in the event of over-watering. They won £1,000 from the RHS and Kew are interested in the idea.

As a further warm-up, here is an example from the author's own experience. The problem was how to water household plants in a courtyard when away on holiday? The commercially available wick materials had failed previously and the author did not want to trouble the neighbours with a watering request. There are electronic water controllers available but there is the matter of the cost and there was not time to purchase one and test it. How would you resolve the problem?

In fact, a word was chosen by arbitrarily consulting a dictionary; this was to act as a stimulant to thinking and to produce a novel perspective – the dictionary yielded the word 'cow'. This triggered the idea of an udder and from that a rubber glove as used for doing the washing up. A drainpipe was intercepted in the courtyard and the rubber glove was tied to the end just above a selection of plants. Each finger of the glove was pierced and a length of sisal was knotted on the inside of the glove and the sisal lead down to the plant pot. You may laugh – but it worked and all the plants survived.

You are recommended to choose a problem statement ('how to …')

from an area that you know well or alternatively, if you want another warm-up try the problem below.

How to scare birds away from your garden or crops effectively but cheaply?

Other issues around the problem are that the solution should not be anti-social – so an excessive use of fireworks or very loud music is unacceptable. You should also be aware that birds are not as stupid as some people think – they get used to regular frighteners, which then cease to provide the desired results. So, how are you going to resolve this? Some ideas for bird scaring:

a) helium filled balloons are fairly effective, but above all are cheap and easy to install and maintain

b) make a pyramid of shiny materials and place this on a 12-volt record turntable to catch the sun

c) arrange for a dummy to be inflated about every quarter of an hour

d) if you can obtain an ultrasonic noise generator, this works well since birds can hear in this frequency range; if you arrange to electronically oscillate the output, this gives the impression of movement

e) set off fireworks at random intervals or fix 12-volt servomotors to the limbs of a scarecrow to produce movement

f) obtain a cat.

In reviewing your ideas ask yourself the following questions: -

● Which parts of the problem solving went well and which parts did not go so well. Why was this?

● Did you apply some problem analysis and definition or did you simply accept the issue as given?

● Did you apply any of the tools as shown in chapter 7?

Oddball and small – but creative !!

Here are a few of my favourites:

● Colombian drug barons disguised their lethal product by coating it with manure and shaping it to resemble excrement.

179

- On a similar theme, there was a Brit held as a Tasmanian convict who collected and then stole the officers' excrement cans. He used these to construct a raft and escaped. It is said that his name was James Turd.

- On a lighter note is the rotatable hat or cowl that fits on your anorak and runs on a form of curtain rail. This enables you to protect your face if you wish.

- A beer to be called 'That' hopes to cash in on the pub habit of occasional drinkers who say 'I'll have a pint of THAT please'.

- If you're fed up with your green lawn, you may be able to grow one that is red, brown, purple or even luminous for night time revels (maybe they heard about the light emitting jelly fish gene). The new colours can be produced by genetic modification and could also kill pests by secreting a toxin from a poisonous fungus. The manufacturers also expect to be able to produce grasses that need little watering or cutting. Perhaps they could even be made to change colour by picking up your mood and ... ...

Creativity is all around us. Make a list of your own favourites and/or areas were you would like to see something new or more helpful. The arts is an area that is obviously creative in its content but Alan Ayckbourn has added something to to the process around his plays. In 'House-Garden' which played in London in February 2000, he combined two plays and one cast with two separate audiences. The stages had to be close together and some actors arrived breathless after stepping through the french window of the 'house' – running between play houses and arriving into the 'garden'. The two audiences were allowed to mix during the intervals and attended the village fete after the play.

If farmers, teachers, administrators and the movers of fast moving consumer goods feel they have not been overly excited by the examples above, here is something for them.

- **Farmers** might be interested in virtual fences. Fences are the old paradigm and electronic control of animals (without fences, which cost up to £4000 per mile) is the new approach. A cow's grazing movements can be controlled by issuing verbal instructions into either ear from small loudspeakers. If the critter does not pay attention a small electric shock can be administered on one side or the other.

- **Teachers** may wish they could control their pupils in a similar way, but unfortunately most parents disapprove and instead motivation is the method of choice. There are working prototypes available of the infrared slate, which allows a more interactive session to be developed in the classroom. Each pupil has an electronic slate, which is in communication with a central screen. Originally developed for mute students, it would also be of value to encourage the fuller participation of the shyer children.

- For **PE teachers,** the snow-board simulator shows the way ahead for learning intricate and subtle body movements. The expert and the student are both wired to a central processor and both stand on snow-boards – in this particular case, on separate but linked snow-boards that are also wired up to detect and direct movements. The instructor leads off and the learner literally feels through the board's movements how the expert is controlling the board.

- The general area of **administration** does not contain a large number of famous innovations, mainly because it is a difficult area in which to take risks and generate a desire for change; however the author applauds the following examples.

  - Needle exchange programmes for drug takers may sound mundane but that is mainly because after the event, most innovations appear fairly obvious and also few of us know how much argument was required to obtain the agreement for the first programme. The old paradigm was to make life difficult for drug takers, and yet to deny them clean needles leads to disease and death.

  - The second administrative example shows how by taking a very different perspective on an old issue – in this case reversing the status quo – can lead to an effective solution. In slum estates, it was always the alleyways between houses that were associated with crime and violence. Estate planners had known this for a long time before they first made some changes on a Scottish housing project. They reversed the pattern of the houses and introduced small gardens between the fronts of the houses with an open footpath running like a spine between the gardens. A cost-benefit study showed that the extra planning effort had paid off by several hundred percent. It is hoped that these illustrations of quite humble innovations demonstrate how worthwhile it can be to summon up the energy to search for a creative solution.

Fast-moving consumer goods (FMCG) are the well known brands that are the life-blood of supermarkets – such as brands of breakfast cereals, kitchen towel rolls, alcoholic and non-alcoholic beverages and confectionery. The history of FMCG illustrates the standard innovation curve of the initial break-through with the novel product followed by variants and the hard grind to reduce costs and improve performance. The history of some brands and some non-FMCG best sellers is illustrated as follows:

- frozen food (Clarence Birdseye) – 1920s
- pre-cooked frozen food – 1930s
- Nestlé's instant coffee – 1937
- the credit card (Schneider and McNamara) – 1950 – it is said that McNamara was motivated into the invention by his acute embarrassment at being in a restaurant without any cash to pay the bill
- the non-stick frying pan using Teflon (Marc Gregoire) – 1954
- frozen fish fingers – 1955
- the Frisbee – 1957
- the Walkman – 1979
- the compact disc – 1982.

The brand producers use advertising a lot to help to market and innovate their products and their advertising houses are some of most creative centres on the planet. As expected, the history of FMCG has illustrated a lot of the tools and art of creativity and innovation. The tobacco industry – especially in the UK since the 1970s – has been hit very hard by government anti-smoking legislation and needed a lot of creative advertising to survive.

In the 1970s, tobacco adverts relied on sports sponsorship – trying to blur an image by relating to a healthy – or at least sporty – life style. The simultaneous attempt at a positive message was that at least tobacco profits were being spent on a worthwhile set of sporting causes linked by television into the heart of our homes. Government pressures relentlessly dogged their footsteps and the adverts and all packaging was required to carry the famous health warning.

Later, tobacco products were forbidden to allude to alcohol, sex or even to 'exciting' images in their advertisements. This must have driven the creative artists crazy and their response was that weird set of very abstract adverts. The idea seemed to be to catch the viewers attention and cause them to pause while they tried to figure what on earth the advert was trying to convey.

Apart from the adverts, some of the most creative outpouring in the FMCG world can be classified under the headings of packaging and products and the latter can be sub-divided into life style, convenience, food and beverage.

Packaging

One of the most famous examples of a package that was deliberately designed from first principles using the methods described in this book was the tetrahedron-shaped pack produced by the Tetrapak company in Sweden and generally used for the transport of liquids – notably milk. The shape is easy to manufacture and approximates to a sphere, which provides the maximum of contained volume for the minimum surface area. Only a part of the power of the innovation was in the shape, the rest remains fairly hidden in the layering of the structure that keeps the intake of spoiling gases such as oxygen within the limits set by the shelf life.

FMCG innovations affecting lifestyle

- The sales of mineral water are testimony indeed to the power of advertisers to produce a market after spotting a trend in the 1980s towards a societal desire for a healthier way of life.

- As soon as Dietcoke, the diet drink, was on the shelves with all the labels lined up facing in the same precise direction, one knew that Pepsimax would not be far behind.

- In a similar way, the sales of organic foods are still rising, helped for example, by the mid-2000 decision by the Iceland retailing company to sell organic vegetables at the same prices as ordinary vegetables.

- Low-fat food was followed by zero-fat food and the flavour chemists were hard at work trying to ensure that our taste buds did not lose out.

- The decaffeination of coffee is now a mass production process involving both the use of solvents to extract the exciting caffeine and freeze-drying techniques to retain as much as possible of the natural flavourings.

FMCG innovations affecting convenience.

- The post-it, developed by 'accident' within the 3M organisation, is a legendary example of how an innovation can flourish against all the odds. Not only did the production chemists say they could not produce the little yellow sticky sheets, but the finance folk said it would not make any money and the marketers said that it would not sell. It has in fact been the single biggest product that 3M have ever had.

- But how many readers have seen or more significantly bought the pre-cut strips of sellotape that are now sold as an alternative to nibbling at a sticky roll with your teeth or sticking sellotape all over the kitchen scissors.

- The drinks can has attracted a lot of innovative attention. It is said that the ring pull opening was produced as a result of using a ripening pea pod as a biological metaphor. Nature arranged to hurl peas a fair distance out of the ripening pod in order to ensure the plant's survival.

  As the pod ripens, the skin thickens along one edge, which creates a line of weakness. As the growing peas put more pressure on the skin, this finally ruptures and flings the peas outwards.

Correspondingly, the carefully judged scoring on the top of a can produces a similar tearing of the metal as pressure is applied through the ring. The gradual improvement of the product now allows the ring to be folded away but retained on the can thus avoiding the proliferation of separated metal rings and a bad image for the can and its product. For beer sold in cans, the cycle did not end there – the so-called widget housed in the bottom of the can dispenses carbon dioxide to imitate draft beer. The extra weight of the can also makes purchasers and consumers think they are getting a higher value product.

● The microwave oven is a great convenience even if elderly users did initially try to dry their dogs inside and similar technological principles should soon see the microwave freezer which is currently being developed by Hitachi. However the microwave oven, after only 20 years, may already be on the way out. Four companies are racing to perfect the next generation household oven. The Jet Direct is produced by the American appliance maker, Thermidor, and uses a technique called jet impingement to achieve very fast cooking rates. Jets of hot air bombard the food at speeds up to 60 mph. The food is smothered in a blanket of hot air and cold spots are virtually eliminated which reduces the cooking times by up to three quarters. Thermidor hoped to have the oven available in the UK during 2000 for a cost of about £3,500.

The key question for the producers is 'just how much will sufficient numbers of consumers pay for convenience'. The other side of the equation is just how much time is a given consumer prepared to spend on a mundane task. The last two decades have seen increasing numbers of women at work and social trends such as more single-parent families and relative prosperity in some parts of the UK have prompted even the sale of pre-washed and pre-chopped salads – unheard of in the 1960s. In 1993, British families spent £840 million on ready meals and by 1998 this had risen to £1.2 billion. The author can also remember his mother boiling the family nappies – now we have 'Pampers' for pampered babies.

FMCG innovations for food and beverages.

- Pringles are like potato crisps but seem to have been cloned from the same mother because they all have the same shape and fit together. How can they afford to sell them in a cardboard tube so that they do not get damaged? Although somehow they have been a commercial success, it is their conception that illustrates a tool of creative problem solving. It is claimed that the metaphor of 'wet autumn leaves' which get packed together by the wind led to the idea for Pringles.

- Thick, condensed Campbell's soup is said to have been thought up by using a random word technique to gain a novel perspective for a new form of soup. The random word used to stimulate the thinking was 'fork' and from this the group imagined they would need to eat the soup. Then someone made the point that the soup could start thick – which had several advantages – but would then be diluted to end up like a conventional soup.

- There was a time when wine was only sold in 75 cl. Bottles – but in California, this paradigm was challenged and the marketing of a range of smaller sizes commenced. An identical process was applied to fruit juices and General Foods also decided to add the convenience of a small straw with a corrugated stem that would bend without collapsing.

- Other recent innovations have been luxury ice-cream, alcopops and tea that used to be sold in large packets and then appeared in round bags and was then stuffed into pyramids by chimpanzees.

Environmentally friendly innovation

Nudging technology towards sustainable development is a complex, value-laden and at times emotional debate and it is not the author's intention to do justice to it here. There are offered instead a few examples of what innovation can achieve with a little more care.

In 1985, the German Green party refused to provide their members of parliament with computers. It was partly a headline catching ploy but their rationalisation was that political problems could not be solved by using industrial technology. However, the use of closed production cycles, energy efficient transport and a start to the phasing out of fossil fuels has shown some ecowarriors that technology can be harnessed to innovate in the service of the environment. Greenpeace argued that publishers should stop using chlorine to bleach printing paper because it was so harmful for the environment. Publishers of course tried to resist the claims and counter-argued that there were no viable alternatives. The Greenpeace response produced a very powerful blend of publicity and common sense – they funded the development of a chlorine-free process which is now in production.

When it was realised that chlorofluorocarbons were having a profoundly negative effect on the Earth's atmosphere via the ozone layer, Greenpeace called for the banning of CFCs in domestic refrigerators. Naturally, the manufacturers said it could not be achieved until Greenpeace converted a factory and did it. They used a former East German factory to produce a commercially attractive alternative called the Greenfreeze refrigerator. The eco-paradigm has changed the world, probably irreversibly and the cases below illustrate how technology is now used to minimise environmental damage, manage fragile ecosystems and devise ecofriendly products and manufacturing systems.

Case 1 – growing petrol

The activity of Bonn's Union to promote oil and protein plants was the main factor that in 1996 enabled German cars to use rape-seed methylester in their fuel. The fuel is now sold at over 800 garages and sales rose from 5,000 tons in 1993 to 100,000 tons in 1997. A derivative of bio-diesel now also heats the new Reichstag in Berlin with the same performance as conventional fuels. It is subsidised by about one US dollar per litre so that the forecourt price equates with conventional fuels. Using this and other measures, it is planned that Germany's carbon dioxide emission from diesel fuels will be cut by 4 percent by 2005. Similarly the Brazilians have been using some of their sugar crop to produce motor fuels since 1990, although it has been argued that this was a move driven by more by a desire to achieve economic substitution rather than environmental protection.

Case 2 – farming by satellite

Some of the technology that was used to bomb Baghdad is now metaphorically being beaten into plough shares. This global positioning data provided by satellites can be used to produce maps showing the distribution of soil types and chemicals, crops, pesticide and herbicide distribution. One of the most interesting sets of data for farmers is that showing the distribution of salinity. The United Nations Food and Agriculture Organisation has estimated that salinity has damaged 35 million hectares of the world's 270 million hectares of irrigated land. In China, almost one quarter of the country's farmland has been seriously degraded by saline deposits. In Californian valleys, salinity is being measured by a machine that carries large electromagnets that create a magnetic field up to 2 metres into the soil. Salts and other chemicals in the ground conduct the small electric currents that result and in turn these currents are detected by sensors fitted to the machine. By comparing local results with GPS maps from satellite reconnaissance the farmers can re-route their irrigation to improve the overall balance of salt concentrations.

11

Tailpiece

As well as writing articles about creative problem solving and innovation the author also offers workshops and more formal 'lectures' about these subjects. These can last anywhere from 2 hours up to 3 days and can be either more serious or more fun – for example, an evening session on a business away-day. It is also possible to engage in real-time problem solving on actual problems – simply turn up with your issue and be facilitated to produce novel solutions. The author has run events in Europe as well as the Far and Middle East and so can cater for different ethnic cultural approaches to creativity and innovation.

When delivering workshops, the favoured approach is action learning in which participants learn by doing. They are required to bring their own problems or opportunities and these are used as vehicles for learning the various problem solving tools. The author has developed 12 work-stations at each of which a different tool is learned.

For more information,
phone: 01326-250970
e-mail: to david.odell@lineone.net
write: 'Trehunsey Vean', Old Church Road,
Mawnan, Cornwall TR11 5HY.

Index

4-diamond process, 24, 73
4P+T, 21
5 Ws + H, 116

Affirmations, 57
Apollo 13 space mission, 14
Attitude, 135
Attribute analysis, 85
Auto-suggestion, 139

Backward chaining, 138
Barnes-Wallis, 167
Bath - ideas in the, 50
Battery-charging footwear, 169
Baylis, Trevor, 61, 84, 152
Belbin team role model, 38
Beta waves, 48
Bionics, 92, 170
Biro, Lazlo, 62
Blockbusters, 79
Blocks to creativity, 147
Bluetooth, 93
Boltzmann, Ludwig, 63
Bones to order, 161
Bouncing bomb, 167
Brain, 44, 136
Brain waves, 48
Brain states, 49
Brainstorming, 106
Brainwriting, 106
BSE and CJD, 10

Cause and effect diagram, 115
Centre for Creative Leadership, 19
CFCs, 187
Champions, 67
Child rearing and parenting, 11
Clashes between individuals, 31
Climate, 65, 77
Clockwork radio, 85, 153
Cognitive mapping, 122

Colours of the mind, 40
Competence, 127, 135
  frameworks, 66
Convergence, 105
Convergent thinking, 15
Corpus callosum, 44
Counselling, 32
CPSI, 18
Creativity, 10, 26, 60, 66, 180
Creativity - definition, 9
Cults, 139
Culture, 65

Dam busters, 55
Dancing with Elephants, 66
Dark night of the innovator, 61
De Bono, Edward, 39
Decision making - definition, 11
Definitions, 9
Dentist, 160
Deviation, 41
Dispersed Note Book, 109
Divergence, 102
Divergent and convergent thinking, 74
Doodling, 46
Double hexagon, 83
Duke cards, 137
Dyson, James, 62, 70, 130, 154

EACI, 18
Ease-value matrix, 122
Edison, Thomas, 60
Efficiency, 31
Einstein, 14, 76, 139
Emotion, 147
Enterprise Network, 157
Ethnic cultures and values, 62, 106, 152
'Eureka' moment, 50, 60
European Association of Creativity and
  Innovation, 128
Extra sensory perception, 136

Eysenck, 18

Fabrics and clothes, 171
Facilitating, 144, 146
Farmers, 180
Farming by satellite, 188
Fast-moving consumer goods, 182
Feelings, 36
Fishbone diagram, 115
Force field analysis, 113
Force fitting, 108
Freud, Sigmund, 14
Future Search Conference, 86

Gallileo-Gallilei, 52
Gandhi, 14
Gender, 35, 45
Golden window, 90, 107
Group conformity, 30
Gut feeling, 17

Herrmann's whole brain approach, 39
Hubble telescope, 14
Huxley, Aldous, 53
Hypnosis, 139

Idea generation, 76
Imagination, 132
Implementation, 124
Incubation of ideas 55, 79
Information technology, 166
Innovation, 10, 26, 43, 52, 66, 81, 130
Innovation Academy, 156
Insight, 132
Institute for the Future, 70
Intelligent clothes, 172
Intuition, 17, 36, 47, 132, 139
Invention machine, 86
Inventors, 151
IQ, 16
Ishikawa diagram, 115

'Jewels', 29
Jewish groups, 69

Kepner-Tregoe, 39-40, 121
Kirton, Michael, 18, 24, 30
Kwolek, Stephanie, 52

Lack of imagination, 148
Learning plan, 128
Left and right brain thinking, 44, 46
Lifestyle, 183

MacKinnon, DW, 37
'Magic cube', 83
Magnetic resonance imagery, 44
Marconi, 52
Matrices, 89
MBTI, 35
Medical patches, 167
Medicine, 159
Meeting plan, 40
Mending bones, 160
Meta-plan, 111
Metaphor, 97, 107
Military conflict, 70
  innovation, 166
Miniaturisation, 166, 170
Mistakes, 177
Morphology, 82
Music, 142
'Musts' and 'wants', 42
Myers-Briggs, 24, 35, 74
Myers-Briggs Creativity Index, 37

Nobel prize, 20, 63
Non-verbal behaviour, 74

Observation of nature, 92
Occupational guidance, 33
Odyssey of the Mind, 19
O'Brian, Dominic, 47
Opportunities, 60
Organisation, 65
Originality, 31
Osborne, Alex, 15
Over-confidence, 148

P for 'press', 23, 65

P for person, 21, 27-28
P for process, 21, 72
P for product, 22, 80
Packaging, 183
Paired comparison, 88
Parents, 11
Pasteur, Louis, 20
Patents, 157, 176
Patterson, Fiona, 43
PE teachers, 181
Peacemakers, 32
Persistence, 60
Personal/cultural perception, 147
Physiology of thinking, 44
Picasso, 14
Playfulness, 61
Polaroid, 54
Post-its, 106
Preferred quaternary mode, 37
Private life, 12
Problem Box, 102
Problem definition, 105
Problem solving, 11
  and its environmental context, 13
Process, 72
Produce your own innovation, 176
Product development, 82
Product improvement check list, 82

Questionnaires, 30, 35, 38, 40, 67, 148

Ranking tools, 97
Reward, 67
Rhodes, Jerry, 40
Rickards, Tudor, 33
Risks, 10
Robots, 163
Roles, 39
SCAMMPERR, 82, 116
Scenario Building, 116
School, 12, 146
Second sight, 137
Sikorsky, Igor, 62
Silver, Josh, 153
Six hats, 40

Smart bombs, 169
Spectacles, 153
Spirituality, 134
Starlab, 70
Stevenson, 53
Stress, 56, 148
'Stretch' targets, 127
Structured Approaches to Problem
  Solving, 82
Style, 27, 31
SWOT analysis, 86
Synechtics, 18
Systems dynamics, 120
Systems thinking, 101

Targets, 127
Teachers, 181
Team roles, 39
The Age of Innovation, 26
Thermodynamics, 62
Thinking, 36
Thinking out of the box, 76
Thriving on Chaos, 66
Thunks, 40
Tobacco adverts, 183
Torrance's fluency factor, 16
Train-the-trainer, 28
TRANSFORM, 82, 116
Trends in product development, 94
Triangle of forces, 98

University, 146
Use of Tools, 96

Vacuum cleaners, 154
Visioning, 86
Visualisation, 57
Visualisation exercises, 140
VOCATE, 99
Voodoo, 139, 169
Voting processes, 88

Walkman, 54
Weak signals, 118
Whole-brained people, 11